Applied Meisner for the 21st-Century Actor

D1195975

Applied Meisner for the 21st-Century Actor develops Meisner's core principles for the contemporary actor and presents a Meisner-based acting technique that empowers practitioners to take ownership of their own creative process.

In this book, the authors present the best, most applicable foundational components of Meisner's technique in a clear, pragmatic, and ethical manner, and advance Meisner's core principles with their own innovations. Drawing on the best practices of consent-based work, they outline a specific approach to creating clear boundaries for the actor and establishing an ethical acting studio. Filled with practical exercises, useful definitions and explanations of foundational principles, and helpful advice on how to recognize and overcome common acting traps and pitfalls, this book provides a replicable and flexible technique that puts the actor at the center of their training.

Applied Meisner for the 21st-Century Actor offers actors and students of acting courses a workable technique that will foster growth and discovery throughout their career.

The text also includes links to the companion website www.21CActor.com, where readers can engage with the material covered in the book and with Otos' and Shively's most up-to-date research, supplemental materials, and training opportunities.

Kevin Otos is a professional actor and director and Associate Professor of Acting at Elon University, North Carolina, where he teaches Acting, Movement, and Period Styles.

Kim Shively is a professional actor and director, Associate Faculty at Theatrical Intimacy Education, and Assistant Professor of Performing Arts at Elon University, North Carolina, where she teaches Acting, Voice, and Content Creation.

Applied Meisner for the 21st-Century Actor

Kevin Otos and Kim Shively

Routledge
Taylor & Francis Group

NEW YORK AND LONDON

First published 2021
by Routledge
605 Third Avenue, New York, NY 10158

and by Routledge
2 Park Square, Milton Park, Abingdon, Oxon OX14 4RN

Routledge is an imprint of the Taylor & Francis Group, an informa business

Library of Congress Cataloging-in-Publication Data
Names: Otos, Kevin, author. | Shively, Kim, author.
Title: Applied Meisner for the 21st-century actor / Kevin Otos
and Kim Shively.
Description: New York, NY : Routledge, 2021. | Includes index.
Identifiers: LCCN 2020053457 (print) | LCCN 2020053458 (ebook) |
ISBN 9780367542719 (hardback) | ISBN 9780367542764 (paperback) |
ISBN 9781003088462 (ebook)
Subjects: LCSH: Meisner, Sanford–Criticism and
interpretation. | Method acting.
Classification: LCC PN2062 .O86 2021 (print) |
LCC PN2062 (ebook) | DDC 792.02/8–dc23
LC record available at https://lccn.loc.gov/2020053457
LC ebook record available at https://lccn.loc.gov/2020053458

ISBN: 978-0-367-54271-9 (hbk)
ISBN: 978-0-367-54276-4 (pbk)
ISBN: 978-1-003-08846-2 (ebk)

Typeset in Stempel Garamond LT Std
by Newgen Publishing UK

Access the Companion Website: www.21CActor.com

From Kevin: For Hannah and Grace

From Kim: For Palmer and Ike

And for our students, who share the studio bravely and inspire us daily to keep learning.

Contents

Part II: Technique **95**

Part III: Additional Considerations **147**

Foreword

I remember receiving a call from a friend once, who was putting together an acting curriculum for a newly created theatre program. "Can I get your opinion on this?" he asked. "Do you think we should throw a little Meisner in there someplace?" It occurred to me that this was like saying about a science curriculum: "Do you think we should teach a little gravity in there someplace?" For my friend, his conception of "a little Meisner" was that it was some sort of special spice that a chef has on her shelf and when she cooks up a Meisner dish she uses the Meisner spice; then when she is finished she puts it away and goes back to the regular stuff. As Kevin Otos and Kim Shively argue in this wonderful book, it is certainly possible to reject the fundamental tenants of Meisner-based work, but it is difficult to understand how principles this radical and transformational (once adopted) could be inconsistently applied to dramatic material. If you accept the basic Meisner approach to acting, there is no going back to "the regular stuff." Or, as we might say about the science curriculum, "If gravity works, it works all the time."

The authors state that their intention is to write a book they wish were available when they were training. Indeed, this is a book that I wish were available when

I was still in the studio working with actors. The extra-ordinary value of this book is that it systematically and with great clarity guides the actor through a Meisner-based methodology from first exercise to beginning scene study. It is important to emphasize the words "Meisner-*based*" because the authors each have their own teaching methodology which is certainly influenced by Meisner but reflects insights and approaches resulting from their decades of teaching experience. In my view this book does two incredibly important things. First, it offers a clear and specific definition of the essential principles of Meisner-based work, illustrated by excellent, well-explained exercises, and second, it creates a dialogue with the reader in which the authors carefully prepare the actor to engage the exercises and then anticipate problems, traps, and pitfalls that often happen. It is as if they are in the studio with the actor to guide them because, well, that is exactly where they HAVE been for a generation teaching graduate and undergraduate actors.

Of course, this is not the first book that identifies Meisner with the reality of doing and the focus on the other. But it is the best one I know for specifically demonstrating why those things are so important. Perhaps the single most compelling contribution made by this book is the way in which they demonstrate their deep understanding of the concept called "Point of View." This concept is not part of what Meisner taught but is what Otos and Shively have adapted from the work on point of view developed by master acting teachers Jim Wise and Robert Cohen. As you will see in the book, understanding point of view completely changes the way we think of character. Character is not something the actor creates in themselves; rather, character is something they create in other people based on their point of view of them. It is always mind-blowing to tell a young acting student that it is impossible for an actor to play their own character. This is true because, as in life, we think of ourselves as "normal" and everybody else as a character. We behave toward them based on the way we think of them and so WE "characterize" THEM. We play to THEIR character. Or as Otos and Shively say: "character exists in the mind of those watching the action."

This exceptionally useful book concludes by applying all this work to scene study from *Uncle Vanya*. The critical stage in any actor training process is the transition from improvisational exercises to scripted material. Otos and Shively handle this beautifully by emphasizing that "a useful way to think about scene work is that you are doing the exercises using someone else's words." Just as it does in the exercises, the book guides the reader through an extensive scene study (as they would in any play) while incorporating everything the student has learned from the first part of the book. Therefore, the reader of this book has what I have never had in my career as an actor and teacher, namely, a comprehensive Meisner-based book that gives the student a way of working from the first day in the classroom to the time when the actor puts it all together in rehearsing and performing in a play. The authors have succeeded marvelously in writing the book they always wished they had.

Brant Pope
University of Texas: Austin

Acknowledgments

Special thanks to all of our teachers, particularly those that made a useful dent. Their knowledge and wisdom are evident throughout these pages.

From both Kevin and Kim: to Jim Wise, Brant Pope, and John Basil, words cannot begin to describe the depth of gratitude we have for all that you've taught us and the creativity you've inspired within us.

From Kevin: thanks go to José Quintero, Lesly Kahn, Sarah Barker, Avner Eisenberg, Julie Goell, Louis Colaianni, Rocco Dal Vera, Pete Henderson, Chuck Slater, and to Jim Kottwinkel, who found the time during our Theatre History independent study to greatly improve my writing skills. Special thanks to Rideaux Baldwin who believed in me when I needed it, and to the irrepressible Christopher Harris who challenged me when I needed that.

From Kim: thanks go to Tom Bradac and Michael Nehring who started it all and instilled a deep love in my heart for community; to Elizabeth Mestnik for the mentoring and teaching along the way; to Lucinda Holshue, Dennis Krausnick, Scott Hayes, Rich Rand,

and Sharon Spelman. And thanks to Barbara Redmond for being an example of consistency and care in the acting studio.

Thanks to all of those who supported and encouraged us in the writing of this book.

From Kevin and Kim: thanks go to our first reader, Susanne Shawyer, thank you for your friendship, your work editing the manuscript, and for always making us look better. Thanks to Hannah Otos for producing our videos and sharing your artistry. Thanks to Tony Spielberg for your masterful photography. Thank you to the faculty, staff, and students at Elon University, especially our Acting family: Fred Rubeck, Kirby Wahl, Kevin Hoffmann, and Susanne Shawyer. Thank you to Kevin Lacey for your equity and inclusion contributions, and to all of our students who have played fearlessly and provided feedback along the way. Many thanks to Phil and the team at the Oak House for serving that first coffee and hosting a thousand conversations. Thank you to the team at Theatrical Intimacy Education for helping us make our acting studios braver spaces and for collaborating with such generosity. Thank you to Valerie Clayman-Pye who helped us through the process of the proposal and introduced us to the fine folks at Routledge. And speaking of Routledge, we owe a huge thank you to Stacey Walker, Lucia Accorsi, and the entire team at Routledge. You made this process exciting and fun.

From Kevin: thank you to my family for their love and support throughout my acting career and the process of writing this book. A huge thank you to my father, Cliff Otos, who has listened and encouraged me through the good, the bad, and the ugly.

From Kim: thank you to my family for your patience, love, and support through the completion of this book. Special thanks to my mother, Kaye Kennedy, who held many things together during this process. And last, but certainly not least, thank you to my husband, Ryan Shively, for your continued partnership and grace.

Introduction

Does the world really need another book on acting?

– The Authors

When we first met, we agreed heartily that the answer was "no." Kim was interviewing for a faculty position at Elon University, where Kevin had been teaching for over a decade. As we sat down for coffee on a freezing morning in between a marathon of meetings and interviews for Kim and classes and rehearsals for Kevin, there was an immediate recognition that can only come from being a part of the same family. Like long-lost siblings, we connected over our shared experiences with our teachers Brant Pope and Jim Wise. Though our times at the Florida State University/Asolo Conservatory for Actor Training did not overlap, we both studied within the tenures of these two influential Meisner teachers. After graduation, we both continued our training and explored other aspects of performance which have also shaped our particular perspectives on theatre and actor training. That February as we wrapped up what would become our first meeting, Kim asked Kevin if teaching Meisner to 18-year-olds really worked. Without hesitation he said yes.

Kim joined the Elon faculty and the following fall sat in on Acting I (the first year acting class in the BFA curriculum) and watched Kevin teach Meisner-based technique. His perspective was fresh, his language was clear, and there was a clarity of purpose to the work. Students were working well, listening well, experiencing impulse, and learning in a way that was exceptional for undergraduate programs. During the following spring, Kevin sat in on Acting III (a sophomore-level acting class in the BFA curriculum) and watched Kim teach a Meisner-inspired approach to character, known as Point of View. She taught clearly and methodically in a way that built upon and clarified key concepts from Meisner's technique. Again, the students responded in impressive fashion, making increasingly bold, impulsive, justified choices rooted in the other actor and connected to high-stake situations. During both semesters we periodically met for coffee to discuss class progress and struggles, and to share our respective pedagogies. We have continued this process into the present day.

Adapting the Meisner Technique for the 21st Century

This book presents a Meisner-based acting technique that can be taught, learned, and which *empowers the actor to take ownership of their own creative process*. We have taken the foundations developed by Meisner in the 20th century and made necessary adjustments for the 21st century. While our core humanity remains the same, the way we experience our humanity and express life has changed considerably. We call this technique *Applied Meisner*.

The Applied Meisner technique is a necessary response to 21st-century realities. We have continued using Meisner's foundational principles and developed a technique that is empathetic, safe, and ethical for the 21st-century actor; a technique that is replicable and flexible; a technique that can foster growth and discovery throughout one's career. This book is for actors, teachers, and anyone interested in the craft of acting. It's for anyone who wants to know more about actor training and is seeking to improve their craft. We have written a book we wish had existed when we began our training.

A Streamlined Approach

Our approach is rooted in traditional Meisner technique, but also reflects the teachings of Brant Pope and Jim Wise. Brant was a student of Manuel Duque, a student of Meisner at the Neighborhood Playhouse before Meisner had developed the full repetition exercise. Jim learned Meisner at the St. Nicholas Theatre in Chicago from David Mamet, who was also a student of Meisner's at the Neighborhood Playhouse. What Jim and Brant had in common were the underlying principles of Meisner's technique without the strict adherence to his full progression. They were not committed to preserving the "purest" version of Meisner's teaching style. They were professionals teaching Meisner-based acting.[1]

Another distinguishing feature of our teachers was that they were not interested in creating or preserving any kind of hero worship. In the 20th century, strict adherence to an acknowledged master-teacher like Sanford Meisner was often an important distinction for teachers and actors, though Jim and Brant were somewhat suspicious of such piousness. We like to think of ourselves as the descendants of these heretics. While we respect those who have carried Meisner's technique into the 21st century and are thankful for their considerable contributions to clarifying terms and continuing to teach Meisner's approach, we have found it useful to omit some long-held exercises and forge a fresh path that is clear, pragmatic, and ethical given our 21st-century realities.

Meisner-based, Not Meisner

Only Meisner taught the Meisner technique. The Applied Meisner technique we teach is rooted in and *inspired* by Meisner's foundational principles. However, if you've had some Meisner experience you may find yourself wondering as you read, "What about this exercise?" "What about *Spoon River Anthologies*?" As we stated earlier, we are the heretics in the world of Meisner. We are grateful for his work and the work of his students who codified it, but we do not feel the need to replicate Meisner. We only utilize the exercises that have shown themselves most useful for our students.

Separating the "What" from the "How": Making Peace with the 20th-Century Studio

When Meisner was developing and teaching his technique, there was a widely accepted belief in the United States that actors needed to break down personal (i.e. emotional) barriers in order to achieve artistic significance. So in addition to teaching acting technique, the teacher also became the demolition manager of the actor's perceived emotional barriers. It was not uncommon to hear people liken the actor training process to being broken down and put back together again. Coupled with the authoritarian power dynamics of 20th-century theatre, the invasiveness of this perspective too often created an abusive environment.

Some behaviors of many master-teachers in the 20th century were problematic by contemporary standards and it can be argued that some of Meisner's confrontational teaching style found its way into the structure of some of his exercises. Still, the principles that Meisner instilled in his students are not inherently problematic. These core elements remain essential for the 21st-century actor.

Virtual Examples

At certain points in this book you will see references to links on our website. We've decided to include some virtual examples to illustrate several of the exercises. In these examples you will see actors engaging in a particular exercise and one or both of us doing some side coaching, which is typical with Meisner exercises. Feel free to set the book down for a couple of minutes and use them when you see them.

Part I
Foundations

Chapter 1
What Is Acting?

It's a simple and often neglected question, maybe because the answer seems obvious. But answering this question and understanding its definition are critical. If we are serious about mastering this craft, we need to know what acting is and what it is not. This will help us focus our training and assess our progress.

When we first ask our students "what is acting?" we hear all kinds of answers – it's emotion, it's being realistic, it's "becoming" a character. Haphazard opinions about parts of acting can distract us from committing to what can actually improve our acting. Meisner's definition of acting has an elegant beauty to it. It is simple, easy to remember, and an excellent point of departure.

> Acting is living truthfully under imaginary circumstances.
> – Sanford Meisner (Meisner and Longwell, 1987)

This definition keeps us focused on what is useful because it tells us what acting is and what it is not. Note that the words "performing," "emotion," and "character" are not mentioned. That is because those things are byproducts of living truthfully under imaginary circumstances; they are not our core concerns. We've found that when there is a problem in acting it can always be traced back to the basics. Fully understanding this definition keeps us focused on where to put our attention.

Acting *Is* Living

What is living? This simple question is the subject of numerous books but for actors it is most useful to understand living as *experiencing* the continuous push and pull of individual moments. Meisner called this the *pinch* and the *ouch* (Meisner and Longwell, 1987, 35). That is, you experience behavior from another person (the pinch) and then respond with behavior of your own (the ouch). This is the pulse of living and it is continually present in our everyday lives.

Real life is fluid and alive. Your acting should be too. Life is full of pinch-ouch or the cause-to-effect reality. That is what we mean by "living."

Pinch-Ouch

Cause-to-effect reality is how most people see and interpret their world. Something happens that then causes another thing to happen. You feel a *pinch* and then you *ouch*. When acting, the pinch must be *experienced* before the ouch can happen. When a pinch-ouch is happening between actors, the audience views the acting as truthful. It is the give-and-take of an alive event. When actors "ouch" without having experienced a "pinch," the moment will not appear truthful because the "ouch" is not *justified* without first feeling a pinch. Listening for pinches, and then responding with ouches is the fluid moment-to-moment life necessary for truthful acting.

There are other terms that describe the pinch-ouch reality: cause-effect, action-reaction, tickle-laugh (also Meisner), and trigger-heap are some commonly used terms. Pinch-ouch, however, reminds us to train viscerally. The cause-to-effect, moment-to-moment reality should be physically *experienced* similar to how you physically experience an actual pinch.

Acting is Living Truthfully

Acting is living *truthfully* as opposed to lying, which also includes omitting parts of the truth. In everyday life you may view withholding certain parts of your truth as necessary or even helpful to your situation and that's your choice. Know that most people do not live their complete personal truth in everyday life. When asked "How are you?" you may often respond with the socially acceptable answer, "good," even though you are having a terrible day. If they get your order wrong at a restaurant, you may be polite to the server while inwardly fuming. These are times when you withhold your truth and society deems it acceptable and even "correct." When acting, withholding any part of your personal, subjective truth in the moment is not useful. Commit to living truthfully within the imaginary world.

Note that there is no mention in this definition of "naturally," "realistically," or "believably." We have observed that when students are consciously or unconsciously trying to accomplish those things their acting becomes flaccid and ordinary – at times almost apologetic. Words like "realistically" tend to dull our authentic edge. Focus on telling the truth, your authentic truth in the moment, and trust that those other things will take care of themselves.

Don't confuse truthful with being necessarily dangerous or reckless. That's not part of the definition of acting either. Respect boundaries.

Acting is Living Truthfully Under

Why the word "under"? Why not the word "in"? They're easy to interchange in Meisner's definition but we've come to appreciate "under" because it implies the pressure that a story's imaginary circumstances put on you.

> They don't write plays about the day nothing happened.
>
> – Brant Pope

We regularly heard this phrase from our teachers while training, and it applies to all good stories. Scripts are written about the day when something special happens – a critical event (or crisis) occurs in a life: life, death, love, betrayal and so on. These crises are not necessarily unpleasant, but they are intense and typically rare in one's everyday life. They are the moments when our dreams or nightmares are about to unfold, are unfolding, or have just happened. As actors we get to live truthfully under this kind of heightened, story-worthy make-believe.

Some examples of the day that something special happens:

- In the classical Greek drama *Oedipus Rex*, Oedipus is the King of Thebes during a plague and all goes wrong in his kingdom.
- In Lorraine Hansberry's *Raisin in the Sun*, Walter works to purchase a home within a racist and segregated society, not a progressive one.
- In Henrik Ibsen's *Hedda Gabler*, Hedda seeks liberation within a sexist marriage rather than one built on equality.

Acting is Living Truthfully Under Imaginary Circumstances

The writer has created the script's *Imaginary Circumstances* or the premise of the story (things like the characters, the conflict, the dialog), but they cannot provide everything. As actors it is our job to read between the lines and imagine additional, useful circumstances that help us justify and fully commit to the imaginary situation. These fully realized circumstances are then brought to life in our acting. We call this *crafting*, and you will learn to effectively craft as you work through this book.

Craft to Care

How you choose to work with imaginary circumstances is very important. The choice is simple: you either choose to make choices that help you care more or help you care less. "Craft to care" is a mantra we use in our teaching. Engage with the imaginary circumstances and craft your choices so that you can more fully care and commit to the make-believe situation.

A predicament of our 21st-century reality is that we are regularly confronted by terrible, sometimes nightmarish events occurring globally and locally. While being aware is part of good citizenship, over time this continuous onslaught of bad news can cause a kind of emotional callousing where we unintentionally cope by learning to care less. You may find yourself thinking: "After all, despite the latest disaster, my kids still need me to take them to practice." This is an understandable habit for coping with the downside of life, but that habit is not useful when acting. "Craft to care." Understand the writer's imaginary circumstances and flesh them out with your imagination to help you care more and fully commit to the situation.

Chapter 2
Studio Guidelines

In the iconic diagram attributed to Stella Adler's visit with Konstantin Stanislavski, the number one principle listed is to "work on one's self." This necessity is still true today.

When Stanislavski was developing what would become "the Method" in the early 1900s he was working with predominantly educated people who came from a certain amount of privilege. The actors he trained were quite homogenous by 21st-century American standards. Even when the "the Method" arrived in the United States, to "work on one's self" insinuated that one enjoyed a level of privilege unavailable to many. Afterall, taking time off from trying to survive in order to pursue lofty endeavors like self-knowledge was a luxury. Today, however, it is widely accepted that every person deserves the opportunity to work on one's self regardless of race, ethnicity, gender identity, sexuality, age, socioeconomic status, and so on. The pursuit of self-knowledge is as important as ever for those pursuing a career in acting.

The Keyboard of Humanity: Your Expanded Sense of Self

Our teacher Jim Wise would sometimes say that each of us had a keyboard within, a metaphor for the possible actions, emotions, and selves within us all. Some of these keyboard keys we know well and bring into our everyday life, others we know and keep private, and others we are totally unaware of. As actors, it is useful to accept that within each of us there are both angels and monsters and everything in between – an infinite number of selves. Jim explained that in everyday life we tend to repeatedly play the middle C key, but that when acting we need to allow greater expression from our entire keyboard. Uta Hagan wrote something similar in *Respect for Acting* using the image of an apple: "But I have to become aware of myself as the total apple – the firm inner flesh as well as the brown rotten spots, the stem, the seeds, the core. All of the apple is *me*" (Hagen, 1973).

Many master acting teachers in the 20th century taught that it was important and absolutely necessary for actors to bring this expanded sense of self into their personal lives as well. Generally, we disagree. Though mastering a craft such as acting (or accounting) will influence a person's world view, we have found it useful to look at acting as more of an athletic event. For example, a boxer does not typically box in their everyday life. Their boxing skills are reserved for training and for the ring. If a boxer were boxing in the grocery store, they would get into a lot of trouble. We've found this useful for students to understand: the aspects of this training that you bring into your everyday life is completely up to you, but you must allow all of your possibilities into your acting. You must bring an expanded sense of self into your work.

The Magic Line: Crossing into a Creative Space

Our teacher Jim often referenced the "Magic Line" between the stage and the audience, between one's creative self and one's everyday self. When you are on the stage side of the magic line you are acting impulsively with a full range of humanity. When you return to the real-world side of the magic line, you return to your everyday social self, which is usually a more inhibited and restrained version of you.

Onstage impulsiveness is absolutely critical to your acting and artistry, and it is a core pillar to Meisner's approach that we'll explain shortly. However, in the real world, poor impulse control is associated with all kinds of behaviors and consequences that you probably don't want. So, similar to the boxer, be impulsive when you are training and acting but leave it on the stage or set. A certain amount of impulse control is necessary for you to function in society. As a responsible adult you can do both.

The magic line is an important threshold. We sometimes mark it with tape as a reminder. Stepping over it allows you to widen into your creative, heightened, expanded stage life. When you cross the line, say "yes" to all of your creative possibilities. Embrace your complete self. Bring your entire keyboard of humanity – even the keys you're unaware of – into your acting.

Truth in Acting

There are at least two kinds of truth in this world: *objective truth* and *subjective truth*.

Objective truth refers to absolute truth. Examples of this kind of truth would be something like gravity or the rate of the Earth's rotation. Objective truth does not change.

Subjective truth refers to one's own sense of truth in the present moment. This is commonly known as an *opinion*. "Green is a good color for you" is Kim's *opinion*, or her subjective truth of that moment. But, if the light in the room were to change, Kim might say "Green makes you look sick" and still be truthful. Though her opinions (or subjective truths) seem to contradict one another, they can both be true. Just not at the same time.

Think of all the different truthful opinions your younger self had of a parent or guardian. At one moment they could be your "best friend" and then later that night become a "prudish judge." Both are true at different moments.

Subjective truth is very important for your acting. Opinions mean everything in the moment but can change quickly. One second your parent can be "super kind" because they seem to understand your angst, then the second they say no, they become the "meanest person ever." Commit completely to your sense of truth. Embrace that opinion can change quickly. Changes in opinion are truthful when they are *justified*.

The Dramatic Imagination

You already have an imagination. Like any kind of skill, you can develop your imagination to serve you in a variety of contexts. There are a number of things a person can do to expand their imagination.

When we talk about developing the dramatic imagination, we are talking about utilizing your imagination in a way that improves your acting. Applied Meisner places a specific emphasis on developing the dramatic imagination rather than exploiting personal memories. The realm of the dramatic imagination is infinite and pliable, while personal memories and experiences are finite and limited.

Learning to use your imagination to springboard off of cold general facts into more specific, embodied, passionate stories is ongoing. We've found it most beneficial to engage your senses through activities like reading, listening, and experiencing life. Watching others perform can be inspiring but do not give into the temptation to imitate or copy. Don't aim to be a secondhand, knock-off brand of somebody else, be you!

Chapter 3
Keeping It Safe

We have found that a few principles and rules to keep us on target and safe are useful for actor growth. They guide us as we train and help each of us feel adequately safe to take risks. Structure helps to foster our artistic growth.

Physical Safety: "Actors Don't Bleed"

Acting does not require you to endanger your personal safety. This is critical if you want to have a long career. A brilliant moment is wonderful, and we want a lot of them in your acting, but a busted knee can last forever. "Actors don't bleed." It's one of the first things Jim taught us.

When we act, we use our imaginations to embrace the heightened circumstances of the story. Our bodies respond to this make-believe the same way our bodies respond to dreams. When acting well we find ourselves in a heightened physical state complete with adrenaline, blood pressure, heart rate, an emotional response, and so on. It is important to understand that actions we consider safe in our everyday life can be dangerous in this heightened state. Be very careful with anything sharp – we recommend that you do not use actual knives, scissors, or glass in any of the exercises in this book. We suggest craft scissors for toddlers and plastic knives and cups when required. No weapons of any kind. We need to create a learning space where it is safe to be impulsive and free. It is easier to be impulsive and trust your acting partner when you know that the props in the exercise are safe, and that everyone in the room is committed to "Actors don't bleed."

Emotional Safety

Each person is responsible for their own boundaries. Personal boundaries are helpful in every aspect of your life and take practice. If you haven't already started to think about or practice having boundaries, the acting studio is an excellent place to start. A boundary is a line that marks the end of something and the beginning of something else. In the acting studio, the magic line is a boundary between your everyday life and your heightened life. There is also a boundary between you and everyone else. You are responsible for your own mental and physical wellbeing.

If we asked you to jump off the roof of our acting studio, you would say no because you could hurt yourself. That is common sense, but it is also having a clear boundary. Because acting involves heightened situations and often has physical touch or other intimate behaviors, it is important to have clear boundaries in class, rehearsal, and performance. We utilize the best practices taught by Theatrical Intimacy Education (TIE)[1] in our classrooms.

Best practices for intimacy in stage and screen acting help our students develop and communicate clear physical boundaries. We utilize these principles throughout our teaching and this book outlines a progression we've found useful. We regularly emphasize the differences between our everyday lives that are real and our creative work where we use the dramatic imagination to create deliberately intense situations.

Boundaries and Consent

Dramatic storytelling is full of intense circumstances, conflict, and heartbreak. It's the day that something special happens. As actors, we have the privilege of being a part of these stories, but it is important to know ourselves when setting our boundaries within the storytelling. It's important to respect the boundaries of others too. Creating a culture of consent takes time, practice, and ongoing communication, but we have found that the acting improves as a result. Plus, it's the right thing to do. The days of a guru teacher taking responsibility for a student's boundaries because they "know better" are thankfully over.

The best practices of Theatrical Intimacy Education continue to develop, but at the time of writing we recommend three core tenants for the acting studio. They are:

1. You are responsible for your own boundaries.
2. Your boundaries are perfect just the way they are (Pace, 2020).

3. There is a difference between crossing a boundary and feeling uncomfortable.

A healthy acting studio empowers you to take responsibility and agency for your boundaries. By regularly voicing your boundaries and consent, the studio becomes a fearless space for creative freedom. If you break a boundary, feel a boundary has been crossed, or see a boundary crossed, say something so that those involved can apologize/forgive and make a plan to move forward so that the mistake doesn't happen again. This is part of the way you take ownership of your creative process (Pace, 2020).

A couple other things we just gotta say:

1. You do not have to recall any kind of emotional trauma in the classroom in order to become an outstanding actor. An ethical acting teacher will not pretend to be a therapist. There is a huge difference between fully investing in the heightened circumstances of the imaginary world and recalling a traumatic experience; chiefly, one is make-believe and the other is not. Work with your acting teacher on acting; work with a trained therapist on unresolved traumatic events and other real-life issues.
2. You can keep your clothes on and still become an outstanding actor. We still occasionally hear about some acting teachers requiring disrobing in class to make students more "vulnerable" or "courageous."

We think that's nonsense. There are other ways to develop vulnerability and courage within yourself if you choose to; even when fully clothed.

We strongly encourage our students to rehearse in groups of three or four and not to rehearse alone in pairs. This helps to keep the work professional outside of class. It is important for you to get together with others to rehearse and work on the exercises outlined in this book. Please use your common sense. Do not rehearse in a bedroom or dorm room, and under no circumstances should you rehearse any intimacy choreography or stage combat without a third person acting as stage manager. This keeps the rehearsal about the acting and draws a clear boundary between your everyday life and your work (Shawyer and Shively, 2019).

Note

1 Theatrical Intimacy Education is a consulting group and educational organization specializing in researching, developing, and teaching best practices for staging theatrical intimacy. TIE is led by co-founders Chelsea Pace and Laura Rikard (Pace, 2020). The authors are grateful for the contributions and impact that Pace and Rikard have made to the field of acting and on our classrooms. Their work on intimacy, boundaries, and vulnerability have been transformative in informing how to achieve a more ethical acting studio. For more information, please visit www.theatricalintimacyed.com

Chapter 4
The Foundations: Other, Doing, and Impulse

Having read the earlier section on Meisner's definition of acting, we're ready to learn three foundational principles in Meisner's technique: The Importance of the Other Person, The Reality of Doing, and Impulse. While these three principles are not unique to Meisner, the way in which Meisner prioritized them in his teaching approach (or pedagogy) was remarkable. He developed the repetition exercise as a means of training actors to embody these principles (Meisner and Longwell, 1987). Repetition is one of the great 20th-century innovations in actor training.

It is important for you to become skilled in these three principles. As we said earlier, when a performance fails to realize its full potential, the cause can always be traced back to the basics. Either:

1. The actor does not understand the definition of acting (what acting is and is not) and as a result has put their attention onto something outside the definition of acting, OR;
2. The actor does not understand or has poor facility with one or more of the basic, foundational principles of the craft.

Principle #1: The Importance of the Other Person

When we ask our beginning acting students what they know of Meisner's work, some will inevitably answer: "repeating!" After they describe the repetition exercise (which we will teach you in the next chapter), we ask "What is the purpose of the repetition exercise?" At that point silence suddenly descends upon the room.

Meisner's repetition exercises have several very important training benefits for actors. One of the first principles to understand and embody is to make the other person the most important person in the scene. Repetition will train you to make the *other person* extremely important in your acting; definitely more important than yourself.[1]

Wait – What? How Can I Act Well if I'm Not Focused on Me?

Remember that plays are written about the day something special happens. It's the day one or a series of intense moments of personal crisis unfold as a worthy story. In moments of crisis the *other person* in the situation becomes extremely important. For example, in your real life when you tell that special someone that you are head over heels in love with them for the first time, your attention is completely on that person: How will they respond? What will they say? And so forth. That other person's behavior, which includes the words they speak as well as their total demeanor, becomes more compelling than your self-conscious thoughts. The importance of the *other person* compels this kind of heightened listening that is absolutely necessary for your acting.

When the *other person* is truly important to you they compel 100% of your attention. When all of your attention is on the *other person*, there is no attention left to watch yourself. This frees you from self-consciousness and that is a critical step in your training because it allows your acting to become more authentic and free.

Freedom from Self-Consciousness

Meisner found that when actors are self-focused, they are likely to doubt, edit, inhibit, or in other ways manipulate their raw humanity, making their performances less truthful and less compelling. We have found this to be the case as well. When the actor is focused on self-generating an emotional response, they cannot live truthfully under the imaginary circumstances because they are manipulating themselves for a purpose outside the definition of acting. Meisner found that fully listening to the *other person* and becoming enthralled with them is a critical step toward truthful acting. It is when an actor is 100% *other focused* that the authentic humanity in that actor can impulsively come to life and be freely expressed.

Love Your Acting Partner

In his book, *Audition*, Michael Shurtleff said, "Every scene is a love scene" (Shurtleff, 1979). There is an element of love for any person that is worth your full attention. This love must be deep enough that the other person deserves to hear difficult truth. This love must be deep enough that they are worthy of humanity: prolonged mockery, unjustified rage, or other kinds of punishment are creative dead ends and incompatible with loving one's partner.

It's also very important that this love for your partner cause you to experience their behavior *personally*. Experiencing what is said and done to you onstage in an extremely personal way helps your acting by causing you to respond more fully to the *importance of the other person*. "Love your partner" insists that you bring your full humanity to a scene. "Take it personally" helps you respond with your full humanity. No one watches a story to see the protagonist "take it like a committee." When you take it personally, the *other person's* behavior "pinches" you in a way that provokes you to impulsively "ouch." That's a big part of being alive in the imaginary world.

Principle #2: The Reality of Doing

Acting is doing. Actors are called actors because they *ACT*. They are not called "emoters" or "feelers" or "transformers." There is truth in doing. Meisner said: "The foundation of acting is the reality of doing" (Meisner and Longwell, 1987, 17). Really doing. Not "faking" or "pretending." If the task is to make a peanut butter and jelly sandwich, then *really* make a peanut butter and jelly sandwich.

You are in charge of what you are doing. No matter how you are feeling you can still wash the dishes. Overjoyed, annoyed, in despair: you can still wash the dishes. Meisner understood that by getting the actor's attention off of themselves and onto the *other person* or the task at hand, the actor would become less self-conscious and behave more impulsively.

Doings can be directed at objects or at the *other person*. *Making a sandwich* is a doing directed at *objects*: bread, jelly, and such. *Impressing* our students with this awesome example demonstrates a doing directed toward *other people*.

You cannot pretend and really do it. You cannot fake it and also do it for real. Meisner's technique insists that you to do it for real.

Emotions Are a By-product

It is important to remember that emotion is outside our definition of acting. Emotions are a byproduct and do not make an actor effective or "good." Don't chase emotion. This can sometimes be a hard pill to swallow, particularly in our current culture of rewarding effortful emotion. A young actor musters up tears in the play and is rewarded for being so "good" because they "could cry." These moments of manufactured emotion might *impress* an audience, but they rarely really *move* them. Whether driven by the actor, director, or teacher, these kinds of emotional manipulations are not truthful and do not produce useful results over the long term. At best, this kind of manipulation produces cliché and tension. As Meisner said: "You can't fake emotion" (Meisner and Longwell, 1987, 87). At worst it can become exploitive, boundary-blurring, or just bad acting. Keep your attention on the *other person* and on the doing. Allow yourself to experience emotions in your work if they emerge. But do not attempt to control your emotions.

There are circumstances that require a character to cry, but there are also ways to do this while empowering the actor to remain truthful. These kinds of demands are what *A Practical Handbook for the Actor* (Bruder et al., 1986, 48) calls externals and they are part of the craft of acting addressed later in this book.

Principle #3: Impulse: The Most Unique Expression of You

Impulse is also a pure expression of the authentic, effortlessly original, one-of-a-kind you. It is what wants to be expressed before any kind of social conditioning kicks in to inhibit or manipulate your unreflective response. It is likely something that adults taught you not to do as a child. And it's a key ingredient for great acting.

Actors do not mentally deliberate and then choose impulses. Actors deliberately create situations that can generate impulses when they place their attention fully on the *other person* and on the activity they are doing.

Merriam-Webster Dictionary defines impulse as "a sudden strong and unreflective urge or desire to act." As actors it is useful to think of impulses as strong and compelled (that is, they are compelled from us) and unreflective – it's what wants to happen before we think. They come from the guts. As Meisner said, "The truth of your instincts is the root of your foundation" (Meisner and Longwell, 1987, 59).

Listening with 100% of your attention on the *other person* opens you up to experience their behaviors personally, in a way that is likely to generate an impulse – that unconsidered, immediate, and effortlessly unique response. Don't pause to consider an impulse but ouch immediately in response to the pinch. Engaging with the *other person* creates impulses.

Meisner placed a premium on impulses in performance. First, they appear spontaneous and life-like because *they are*. They look like the event is happening for the first time even though the show may have been playing for weeks because the unique events of that particular performance are unfolding moment-to-moment in real time. Impulses are the spark of life that compel the writer's dialog and motivate the director's blocking. When actors behave impulsively, they are fully invested in the other person and completely free of self-consciousness. Rather than imitating an idea of a past event or judging their impulses in any way, impulsive actors *give over* to the now present moment. Impulse is the most authentic and specific action in acting. It makes the acting alive.

You must nurture your impulsiveness. Since impulses are free and unpredictable, they feel surprising, exciting, and sometimes even dangerous. They are critical not only to your acting but to your total creative development. Improved impulsiveness is one of the key benefits of training with the repetition exercises covered in this book.

Note

1 In the Meisner technique the other person on stage is often referred to as the *other*. When first defining POV, the term *other* was used in *The Players' Journal* article. Since this time, the authors have tried to distance themselves from the term as the weight it holds in our society is in direct contrast to our mission of creating an inclusive, collaborative acting studio.

Chapter 5
The Basic Repetition Exercise

You have committed yourself to learning the craft of acting and in order to do this, you must have a strong foundation. The repetition exercise is one of Meisner's great contributions to actor training. It will instill in you this strong foundation. It will train you to become more truthful, authentic, and free in your acting. It is also the first exercise in a sequence, so you must commit yourself to learning the basic repetition courageously and impulsively.

It's important to remember that these are exercises, not performances. These exercises will reveal your strengths and weaknesses while sharpening your skill in the foundational elements discussed earlier. Just like an athlete cannot perfect wind sprints, you cannot perfect the exercises in this book. There will always be room for improvement. The pursuit of perfectionism will always leave you empty, but in artistic endeavors it's straight-up destructive. Embrace the journey rather than rushing to a result. As we heard the gifted teacher John Basil once say: "look for progress, not perfection." As you move into the exercises, release your need to achieve anything. Rather, give yourself over to what these exercises will teach you.

The basic repetition exercise is the first building block in Meisner's technique. Its rules are simple, but the impact is transformative.

How

Stand opposite your acting partner in an open position on the stage side of the magic line. "Open position" means that your hands are relaxed at your side and you have opened yourself to the possibility of *listening with your blood*, as Stella Adler would say (Adler, 1989). When we stand in an open position, our head, chest and hips are neutral and released and our knees are soft. This is a position that is ready for possibility. It can also feel very vulnerable. You are training for high stakes situations that require vulnerability. Remember, when you cross the magic line, you are saying yes to experiencing and expressing a deeper range of your truth than you do in your everyday life.

Repetition will train you to listen. Listening is a state of doing that goes much deeper than hearing. You must listen to the *other person* with your entire body. It can be helpful to think of breathing them in. This receptive listening, or taking your partner in, is essential for responding truthfully.

Place your attention *gently* on the other person. Remember, you love this person and there is an expectation that they love you. Love is necessary for the person to compel truth from us, even uncomfortable truth.

Already at this starting point we begin with a simple point of view on the other person. "Who do you see?" "I see Kevin whom I love." So, in this example Kim is not pretending that Kevin is different than he is, she is accepting him as he is – looks like Kevin, sounds like Kevin – but is enhancing the everyday relationship by adding the imaginary element "I love." Kevin does the same for Kim – looks like Kim, sounds like Kim – but enhances their everyday relationship with "I love." Because loving has no end, no matter what one's relationship is in "real life," the imaginary world can always be richer.

One person begins by stating an objective truth: "You're wearing a black dress." Without pausing, the other person repeats *exactly what they hear*, but changes the pronoun to "I" so that it represents their truth: "I'm wearing a black dress." The two actors continue to repeat exactly what they hear, changing the pronoun:

Kevin: You're wearing a black dress.
Kim: Uh, I'm wearing a black dress.
Kevin: *Uh*, you're wearing a black dress.
Kim: *Uh*, I'm wearing a black dress.
Kevin: You're *wearing* a black dress.
Kim: I'm wearing a black dress?
Kevin: You're wearing a black dress.
Kim: I'm wearing a black dress.

In this sample exercise, we repeated exactly what we heard. When Kim made the "*Uh*" in response to Kevin's first statement, Kevin repeated it, because he was repeating *exactly* what he heard. Kim then repeated what she heard and Kevin's next response dropped the "*Uh*" because his new impulse made its way onto the dress. This "*Uh*" was most likely a moment of self-consciousness on Kim's part, but this "mistake" is actually the truth of the moment which Kevin accepted by repeating it. Repeating exactly what you hear trains you to respond to what is really happening.

At this point in the process, you should repeat with your partner for about an hour at a time, pausing every 1–2 minutes before placing your attention gently back on your partner and begin again. If you begin to get tunnel vision, stop, shake it off, exhale, place your attention gently on the other person, and begin again. You can repeat sitting or standing, though we have found that there are more possibilities when standing.

Why

Repetition trains you to really listen. Listening is key to living in the moment onstage because when the moment changes you must change. Like in the example when Kim said "*Uh*," Kevin didn't ignore it, he continued to repeat exactly what he heard. This *giving over* to the other person allows them to take you on the journey of each particular exercise. Repetition trains you to *listen and respond* to what is actually occurring in real time.

Repetition further trains you to quiet your self-conscious thoughts because you can repeat a simple phrase without "thinking." The phrase can be reflexive and there is no pressure to consider, deliberate, or "act." Placing your full attention gently on the other person and repeating exactly what you hear is the first step in learning to quiet your mind and act impulsively. The simplicity of this exercise can fool you into thinking that it is easy or boring, but don't be deceived. It is incredibly challenging and requires practice.

Traps and Pitfalls

1. Are you repeating exactly what the other person has just said? If not, you are not truly listening but rather indicating listening. This includes anything that may seem like a "mistake." In the example, when Kim said the "*Uh*," Kevin continued to repeat exactly what he heard because it was the truth of that moment. The words "perfect" and "good" are not part of our definition of acting; the word "truthful" is. It is the truth that matters.

2. Are you speaking before your partner has finished? If yes, you are anticipating the future which is not useful to your acting. Live each moment fully. Though a phrase may be repeated ten times, it is a new experience each time. If the phrase were a kiss,

experience each kiss as a unique event rather than one in a series. Anticipating is an attempt to control the moment. That is harmful to your acting. Better is to cultivate the habit of allowing the moment to control you. Like a current in a river, let the moment take you.

3. Are you mimicking your partner's tone? If yes, then you are manipulating and disguising your truth. Listen for your partner to pinch you (whether that pinch is very slight or incredibly profound), and then ouch on your impulse, repeating those same words. Your truth at any particular moment could be extreme or mundane. If you are afraid of being perceived as mundane you are not alone, but remember that the word "entertain" is not part of our definition of acting. Commit to living truthfully in the exercise. Dare to be boring.

4. Are you pausing? If yes, then you are thinking too hard. Your inner perfectionist might be causing you to be too cautious. Speak before you think and don't try to get it "right." Yes, it is exactly the opposite of what you were taught as a child. "But I don't know what might come out of my mouth!" Right, no one does. And that is what can make your acting so exciting.

5. Are you fixing or ignoring "mistakes"? Sometimes when we feel like we've made a mistake or see a mistake, we have an immediate urge to fix it or ignore it. Neither of these habits serves your acting.

The mistake is simply your humanity. It is the new moment and you must respond to it. People tend to think they are sweeping the mistake under the rug, but what they are really doing is denying the moment. This is a well-trained social habit that must be squashed.

6. Are you asking questions? Repeating is about telling the truth. It is not about passive aggressive questions. "Are you really going to wear that tie?" is a less truthful way of saying "You look ridiculous." In this exercise questions are a form of avoidance. Keep your attention on what the other is *doing* to you and tell the truth. If a question is asked during the repetition exercise, *work off* of that behavior which we will describe in the next section.

Establishing Boundaries

Physical touch is not required at this point in the exercise and we establish that boundary with our students. Your focus needs to be on listening to the other and experiencing the impulses they compel from you. Adding touch at this point runs the risk of overwhelming one with too many impulses and that would muddy your responsiveness.

An example is available on our website. Please visit www.21CActor.com and click on Exercises.

Moving Forward: Working Off of Behavior

As you continue with the basic repetition exercise, allow yourself to breathe as you place your attention gently on your partner. This will help you experience your partner more fully. As you find ease in listening and responding truthfully, you can move the exercise forward. Give your partner and yourself permission to voice the first thing you notice about the other actor. What compels you the most right now? When you give it voice, how does it change your partner?

Dare to be more truthful with your first statement. Rather than "You're wearing a black dress" (irrefutable fact for 99% of people), you may really want to say "Your dress looks great." At which point your partner would repeat exactly what they heard changing the pronoun, "My dress looks great."

By voicing your clear opinion, your subjective truth, your acting enters a place of more passion and possibilities. Voicing a truthful opinion feels like a risk because it is. Your words might pinch (or tickle) your partner and then they will ouch (or laugh) and then you have to work off of their behavior. Your acting will become more truthful, and alive as a result. It's more fun too. *You've got to have an opinion.* A good mantra to have.

A clear, strong opinion is dramatically useful because we have opinions about things we really care about. Opinions are our personal truth of the *right now moment*. So, you recall in our discussion earlier, an actor can choose to craft to care or not. Having a clear opinion on someone or something is part of crafting to care.

Is your opinion justified? If you are making outrageous statements such as telling someone you like their dress when they're wearing slacks, then you are trying to "entertain" and that is not part of our definition of acting.

Now, it is possible that the two actors do not share this opinion.

Kevin: Your dress looks great.
Kim: My dress does not look great on me.

      Or we can take a step into a larger world and label behavior:

Kevin: Your dress looks great.
Kim: You're flattering me.
Kevin: I'm flattering you?
Kim: Yeah, you're full of it.

In both examples, Kevin thought the dress looked great. That was his truth in the moment. Kim hated the dress and that was her truth. In both examples, the subjective truth was a starting point for the exercise. But in the second exercise, it was Kevin's *behavior* that elicited Kim's response, "you're flattering me." That is the normal progression of repetition.

Beware Social Habits – Be Interested, Not Interesting

Once you and your partner begin repeating and working off behavior, you may begin to notice your everyday habits slipping into the exercise. These habits are part of your social self and can inhibit you on the creative side of the magic line. Things like constant smiling, saying "hello!" and persistently trying to be clever or quirky are social habits and aren't connected to what your partner is doing to you. Get interested, get enthralled in the *other* person and what they are *doing*. Don't try to be interesting. Dare to be truthful even if you're afraid that truth is boring!

Remember the Love

Committing to your truth on the stage side of the magic line is necessary for your acting to improve. It is part of learning to "live truthfully." But living truthfully doesn't mean we all become assholes when acting. Remember that you are relating to your partner "that you love." This isn't to say that we are never angry or frustrated with our partner. We can even be mean to them on impulse when we need to get their attention. But prolonged, unjustified cruelty or punishment toward people that we love is not truthful. It's just a rebellion against social conventions by insistently being mean. That's outside of our definition of acting.

An example is available on our website. Please visit www.21CActor.com and click on Exercises.

Chapter 6
The Independent Activity

The Independent Activity exercise is the next important step in learning the Meisner technique. It trains you to put your attention into a physical activity by committing to the reality of doing. In Independent Activity #1 you will be acting alone. You will also begin to practice using your dramatic imagination in your crafting. This requires you to create an imaginary circumstance that contains some relatable truth. In subsequent activity exercises we will add your acting partner.

Independent Activity #1

How

Start by selecting a physical activity that you can do alone and that will take at least 10 minutes to complete. It should require 100% of your attention and be difficult for you to do. This difficulty should not require any "pretending" but simply be genuinely difficult to complete when really doing it. If the activity is too easy, it will not require 100% of your attention and you're likely to become self-conscious. However, if your activity is truly impossible to complete, your *common sense* will not allow you to fully commit to really working to complete it. You need to choose something that is *both difficult and achievable* within a certain amount of time.

These three elements will help you *craft* an Independent Activity with a reasonable level of genuine struggle.

1. You need to know *exactly* what your finished activity will look like. This is called a *cap* (Bruder et al., 1986, 13–14, 17). The *cap* is the specific criteria that must be met for you to be completely finished with the activity.
2. You need to craft the *pressure of time* so that there is just enough time for you to achieve your cap, but not a minute more.
3. You must have a reason for doing the task so that the activity is *justified*.

But Wait, There's More ...

First, you are learning to commit to the reality of doing, so it is important at this stage of your training that you use real props. It is also important that you choose an activity that you generally understand, but that you are not expert in. Again, you want the activity to be genuinely difficult but not impossible.

Next, though we expect that you will present this exercise in a classroom in front of several people, you should imagine that you are completing this activity in a place of *privacy*. When we're totally alone we are less self-conscious and as a result our behavior tends to be more expressive, authentic, and truthful. Use your imagination to set your activity in your bedroom, apartment, or other place where you could reasonably expect complete privacy. This kind of "public solitude" (Meisner and Longwell, 1987, 43) is important for your acting.

Let's review and then go over an example. Is your Independent Activity:

1. Something you can complete alone and in privacy?
2. Something that takes at least 10 minutes to complete?
3. Something you have or can easily get the necessary props for?
4. Within your general understanding?
5. Genuinely difficult to accomplish so that it requires 100% of your attention?
6. Something that has a clear cap that you are working toward?
7. Something that has a reasonable pressure of time?
8. Justified?

Example

(Kevin assembling and frosting a cake for his nephew's birthday party)

Kevin is using his dramatic imagination to craft a situation using a general relationship he understands and can relate to. He does have two real nephews and can identify with the importance of those relationships, but this particular relationship and events are fiction and live in his dramatic imagination. As he crafts the activity, he goes through the checklist:

1. Something you can complete alone? Yes.
2. Takes at least 10 minutes to complete? Yes. Since our acting studio doesn't have a working oven, I will bring in pre-baked cake layers, the appropriate frostings, and other necessary props.
3. Something you have or can easily get the necessary props for? Yes. I have cake pans, mixing bowl, plastic utensils, and a Batman image printed from the Internet. I will need to purchase the cake ingredients (a couple of box cake mixes) and do some baking at home ahead of time so that the layers of cake are ready for assembly.
4. Within your general understanding? I've assisted on a couple of cakes and generally trust my drawing skills for the Batman frosting if I'm copying from an image. I think I can do it.
5. Genuinely difficult to accomplish? Yes, if it is to look good enough for a child's birthday party. Though I have some experience making cakes, I am not a skilled baker. I think this will require 100% of my attention.
6. Have a clear cap that you can really work toward? Yes. It needs to be a party-worthy Batman cake for a seven-year-old and our extended family. The Batman needs to look pristine, like the image I have printed off of the Internet. My nephew's

name will be in cursive light blue writing, which is his favorite color.

7. Have reasonable pressure of time? Yes. I need to have this finished before my sister brings him over to celebrate his seventh birthday with my side of the family. It is currently 2:02 pm and they are due to arrive at 2:30 pm. I believe this gives me just enough time.

8. Justified? Yes. Batman is a special connection between my nephew and me. I haven't been able to see him much lately because we've all been very busy. Homemade cakes are a birthday tradition in my family. This cake is my chance to show him that I love him very much and that I haven't forgotten about him or our special Batman connection.

With this kind of crafting, Kevin can accept the imaginary circumstances and get fully enthralled in the reality of doing. By fully committing to really accomplishing the Independent Activity, you will experience the freedom from self-consciousness that you need for authentic acting.

Traps and Pitfalls

Below are some common problems we see people encounter when learning the Independent Activity. Understand that anything worth learning is difficult, and that setbacks and struggle are part of the learning process. Below are a handful of the many regular difficulties we see people experience with their first Independent Activity.

1. The Activity didn't really require 100% of your attention. You have chosen something that isn't physically difficult enough and you inadvertently made an easy choice. The problem with ease is that it leads to self-consciousness or, even worse, "pretending" that something is difficult when it isn't. Pretending is not part of our definition of acting.

2. The Activity was too "outside" of your general understanding. Did you choose safe cracking or building a jet engine? It can be tempting to choose something way outside of your general understanding, but unless your last job was with MI6, in aerospace, or similar, don't craft an activity to defuse a bomb, build a satellite, or blow glass.

3. Was your Activity capable of being done? Losing five pounds in the next ten minutes might sound good but it never works. First, it might require exertion, but it doesn't require 100% of your attention. Second, it isn't possible, and your common sense will prevent you from fully committing. Both lead to self-consciousness which is the major obstacle to impulsiveness. You want as much impulsiveness in your acting as you can get.

4. Did you try to focus on an emotional obstacle while working on the activity? Emotion can be a tempting tryst, but feelings are fickle and outside of your

control. Think of emotion as a by-product, like steam off of hot water. Commit to the reality of doing and living truthfully under the imaginary circumstances. Whatever feelings you have or don't have are the truth of each moment. Accept them when they're there but don't manipulate yourself by insisting that you feel a particular way. That path is outside our definition of acting and will not serve you.

An example is available on our website. Please visit www.21CActor.com and click on Exercises.

Activity #2: The Walk On

Begin the same as Activity #1 with you doing an Independent Activity. After a couple of minutes your partner will cross the magic line onto the stage. Your partner will then place their attention gently on you and begin the repetition once they experience an impulse to do so. Continue your activity as the two of you repeat, just as you learned in the Basic Exercise. You will place 100% of your attention on the genuinely difficult activity and 100% of your attention on your partner that you love. While repeating, you will feel your attention *torn* between the activity and your partner. It is in this place of conflict that impulse is born. This can feel new and exhilarating, sometimes even a little scary. Allow it to charge you. It is a time-tested generator of impulses.

Helpful Reminders

1. For the Walk On, be sure to give your partner doing the activity a couple of minutes to become immersed before crossing the magic line.
2. For the Activity Actor, know that it is normal to feel your attention shift periodically from partner to activity, back to partner, and so on.
3. Remember to *love your partner.*
4. Respect boundaries and practice consent (explained shortly).
5. Keep your attention on what your partner is *doing to you* and what it provokes you to *do.*
6. Avoid asking questions and other social chit-chat such as "What are you doing?," "Not bad," "Hello," and so on. If questions or chit-chat occur, work off the behavior as explained earlier.
7. Beware of *Social Habits.* As stated earlier, social habits are not impulses, they hide real impulses.

Example

Kim: What are you doing?
Kevin: You asked me a question.
Kim.   I asked you a question.
Kevin: You're confused.
Kim: I'm confused.

In this example, Kim asks Kevin a question, which can potentially derail the repetition exercise. Instead of engaging with the question, Kevin names the behavior, which is asking the question.

Traps and Pitfalls

1. Falling into questions and social chit-chat. Keep your attention on what the other person is doing and how the other person is feeling.
2. Abandoning the activity. If your partner is consistently more compelling than your Activity, then you need to craft and justify a more important activity. Commit to the reality of doing.
3. Losing your love for your partner. If you find the activity so enthralling that your partner is relatively easy to ignore, then you are not loving your partner sufficiently. Commit to the importance of the other.

An example is available on our website. Please visit www.21CActor.com and click on Exercises.

Establishing Boundaries

Once you and your partner begin working with the Independent Activity, there is the possibility that the Walk On may have an impulse to make physical contact with the other actor or the actor's props. Again, we want our work to be as free and impulsive as possible and we find that using the self-care cue (we use the word "button"), explained in *Staging Sex* (Pace, 2020, 17), gives you the freedom to pause the exercise or tell your partner that they are crossing a boundary.

There is an important distinction between crossing a personal boundary and justified behavior that provokes the other person and makes them uncomfortable. The self-care cue is simply a word that doesn't hold the same charge for actors as "Hold" or "Stop," but which can offer a pause in the action, like a breath. This allows the actor to clarify their boundary or refocus the exercise in an effective way without interrupting the action. While the self-care cue could be seen as a disruption, we have found that it actually allows the actors to continue in the exercise without stopping.

This self-care cue is rarely used in the studio, but by always offering the option, we have found that actors are more likely to speak up in moments when someone may be crossing a boundary. If Kim steps into Kevin's space, Kevin may say, "button," because Kim is crossing a personal boundary. We see that actors who regularly work with consent-based practices might use "button" in the exercise, but more often they will be quick to say, "You're crowding me," "Don't touch my things," or "Back off!" Either way, allowing for the self-care cue reinforces that following impulses is allowed, but also that actors don't bleed, and the studio is a brave place that practices good boundaries and consent. In our experience, these boundaries make the space more daring and freer for impulses to flow.

Activity #3: The Knock at the Door

At this point in the exercise one person is onstage doing an activity and their partner will come to the door and knock. The person in the room ("Activity") will go to the door when they have the impulse and are compelled to do so, open it, and label the knock: "angry knock," "timid knock," "crazy knock," and so on. The person at the door ("Door") then repeats that phrase, launching both of you into repeating.

How

Decide who is in the room doing the activity, hereafter referred to as "Activity," and who will knock on the door, hereafter referred to as "Door." It is useful to give "Activity" at least two minutes to immerse themselves in their activity before knocking. The more engrossed "Activity" becomes in what they're doing the better.

"Door" needs to craft the tangible thing they are coming over for that *justifies* their knock. At this stage in the training it is very important that "Door" come over for something that is clearly a physical object: a "cup of sugar" or "dress shirt" rather than "an apology" or "to make a new friend." Continue to get in the habit of justifying your behavior onstage. For now, avoid justifications that are super high stakes or extremely urgent: "I'm coming over to borrow a blanket" is more useful right now than "I need your fire extinguisher, my lover's on fire!" or "Give me your EpiPen!"

At some point the need to complete the activity will compel "Activity" to return to their task.

Example

Kevin: (*As he opens the door*) Angry knock.

Kim: Angry knock.

Kevin: Angry knock.

Kim: Angry knock?

        (*Kevin rushes back to decorating his nephew's cake. Kim walks into the room*)

Kevin: Angry ... (*He stops talking as a challenging bend in the frosting compels his complete attention*)

Kim: You're in a hurry.

Kevin: I'm in a hurry.

Kim: You're frustrated. (*As she closes the door*)

Kevin: I'm not frustrated.

Kim: You're making a cake. (*Walking toward him*)

Kevin: I'm making a cake.

Kim: It looks awful.

Kevin: It looks awful?

Kim: Yes, it looks awful.

Kevin: You don't know what you're talking about.

Kim: I do know what I'm talking about.

Kevin: You're a know-it-all.

Traps and Pitfalls

1. "Activity," are you anticipating the knock? If so, get more involved in the activity. You want to be totally engrossed in it. The character doesn't know that someone is about to knock. Also, since you cannot control the future, you don't know for sure when your partner will knock. So, commit to what you are doing. This way the interruption that the knock creates will truthfully pinch you.

2. "Activity," are you pausing before labeling the knock? If so, embrace your first impulse as you open the door. Remember that these first words label the behavior of the knock. They are not about your partner. Because you cannot predict the future, you do not know for sure who is coming through the door.

3. "Activity," are you coming to the door before being compelled to do so? Opening the door is the "ouch" to the "pinch" of the knock. If you open the door before experiencing the impulse to do so, then the move to the door is unjustified and will not appear truthful. Feel the pinch of the knock before crossing to the door. If you do not feel the pinch of the knock, trust that "Door" will find a way to get you there.

4. "Door," are you embellishing the knock? If yes, you are trying to entertain us and that is not part of our definition of acting. It can be tempting to "help" your work through embellishment. Unfortunately,

these embellishments don't help. They hinder the work and make it appear or sound dishonest because it's not justified. If you are coming over for an egg so you can bake a box cake for your nephew, knock like that, not like you're trying to save the world. Commit to living your part of the story as honestly as possible.

Advanced Version

Raise the importance of the thing that "Door" is coming over for. There is a lot of territory between coming over for a "cup of sugar" and coming over for the "launch codes that can save the Earth." A homework assignment? Your purse? Your favorite outfit? Your dad's car keys? Your grandmother's wedding ring?

An example is available on our website. Please visit www.21CActor.com and click on Exercises.

Activity #4: Expectation and Crafting for Surprise

Now it is time for "Activity" to craft for *expectation*; that is, crafting for reasonable surprise. What this means is that you are crafting a simple justification of who you *expect* to be coming to the door. When "Activity" opens the door, "Door" is not the person they expected. This discovery ignites the first moments of the repetition.

A sample *expectation* could be:

- The delivery driver bringing my dinner;
- A roommate coming back because they forgot their phone;
- A neighbor coming to borrow a cup of sugar.

Actors must have a reason for everything they do. Continue getting in the habit of justifying your crafting. Your justifications should bring you deeper into the imaginary world. *Justification* and *Expectation* are the lighter fluid for the effective fire of your impulses.

Moving Forward

Craft an expectation that makes you "do." This will further inspire actions and impulses. Some sample expectations that make you "do" could be:

- My research partner coming over for the USB drive for our presentation for class. I hand them the USB drive when I open the door.
- I am playing a prank game with my neighbor. I am expecting them to come over for dinner and I have a water balloon ready to throw at them when I open the door.
- I have had a fight with my neighbor, and they are coming by to pick up a board game they left at my house. I expect to hand them the board game and shut the door in their face.

- I'm expecting my one-night stand from last night to drop by to pick up that article of clothing they left this morning. Expect to hand them their clothing at the door.

An example is available on our website. Please visit www.21CActor.com and click on Exercises.

Chapter 7
Common Struggles and How to Work Through Them

As you delve into the work, you are likely encountering challenges beyond the traps and pitfalls we list at the end of the exercises. Perhaps some patterns of struggle are emerging. These fall into the category of *bigger acting problems*. While it's important to deal with them, understand that these are issues most actors will encounter. Don't be discouraged; be happy that you're doing the work necessary to improve. As we said earlier, when acting goes wrong it is often due to a problem with the basics.

We never perfect our art. We just keep working toward more truthful and freer acting. Below are three common struggles people often encounter throughout the training process.

Bigger Acting Problems

1. Fear. You are afraid. Afraid of being wrong. Afraid of seeming foolish. Afraid of looking ugly. Afraid of offending your audience or your acting partner. The best way we've found to overcome this kind of fear is to embrace it by deliberately moving

into the discomfort. If you've established a solid level of trust with your acting partner, share your challenge. You'll most likely discover that you are not alone in your fear. Then take part of that rehearsal to do the repetition exercise with the goal of daring to be wrong, foolish, ugly, offensive, and so on. Once you've finished your rehearsal, you'll notice that you're still alive, your acting partner still supports your efforts, and that you are likely more confident and capable of fully giving over to the exercise. Commit to fearlessly expressing your truth.

2. Perfectionism. You want to be "right." The need to be "right" can be crippling for the actor. There are a couple of different ways to combat this common pitfall. The need to be "right" is another way of saying "I'm afraid to be wrong." See above for our advice on Fear. But also, ask yourself what is "right"? Upon examination what most people picture as "right" is actually cliché. *Cliché* is a shadow of truth that is not unique to you. Cliché resembles some generic version of your truth. If your truth is an egg, cliché is a manufactured plastic egg. Remember, when you give over to the *other person* in the exercise, they become the cause of all resulting impulses and behaviors. Rather than focusing on being right or wrong, commit to speaking your truth. Get enthralled in your partner. Experience the deepest mysteries of the *other person*. You'll have more fun

than when you are worrying about yourself and your acting will likely improve.

3. Control. You want to control yourself. You want to control the *other person*. You're afraid that if you don't control yourself or the *other person*, that you or your partner will do something that isn't "right." Look at the previous section on Perfectionism. But also, examine your desire to control. Do you really believe you can control another person? If you really could, would you want to? What would such a predictable life look like? Would you really want to take total responsibility for someone else's acting? Know this: Any sense of control you have over another adult is a comforting illusion at best and not creative. You *can* control yourself, but no one goes to the theater or movies saying, "Oh goody I get to watch the actors be control freaks for the next 100 minutes." People go to theater and movies to experience the events that cause a person to *lose* control. So, set a personal goal in your next rehearsal to lose control. Be sure to share your goal with your partner to give you both additional permission and ease. Remember, actors don't bleed so use common sense and recognize the boundaries of the rehearsal space. Allow yourself to act outside of the restrictions you have unintentionally created for yourself in the exercise. Dare to lose your shit. Dare to be free. Don't be careful. Be fearless.

Chapter 8
The Foundations Developed, Part I

Further Developing the Technique: POV/Need/Action

When you begin learning Meisner technique, you focus on the foundational principles of other, doing, and impulse. The repetition exercise and independent activities are designed to train you to respond impulsively. These impulses are an organic byproduct of being focused on your doing (the activity) and the *other person*. Meisner himself said: "the practitioner is somebody who is learning to funnel his instincts, not give performances" (Meisner and Longwell, 1987, 37). He went on to explain: "My approach is based on bringing the actor back to his emotional impulses and to acting that is firmly rooted in the instinctive" (Meisner and Longwell, 1987, 37). Making the *other person* important and really doing the activity create the conditions to spark impulses.

This training creates useful habits. It creates psychophysical habits that encourage the actor to behave instinctually. Think of walking through a deep, fresh snowfall. Those first steps are challenging because you are creating a new path. When you walk back through the footprints, it gets a little easier because there is a path to follow. You have created a *rut*, or a habit. As you practice the exercises, you deepen the ruts that lead to impulsive acting.

You have learned about the importance of the *other person*, the reality of doing, and impulse. Doing the exercises in this book has taught you to embody these principles – to create psycho-physical ruts. This section prepares you for scene work by further developing these principles.

They develop in the following ways

- Other –> POV
- Doing –> Need
- Impulse –> Action

Point of View: Crafting Relationships

Point of View (POV) is a Meisner-based way of defining relationships. It is a significant part of the technique. It is essentially crafting how to perceive the other. Everyone has specific POVs that can provoke behavior. That is, when you have a clear POV on someone, their words and actions can pinch you more profoundly, causing you to impulsively ouch. Here's our definition of POV:

> A highly specific, emotionally evocative phrase that encapsulates the lens through which a character views their world, their situation or their other.
>
> (Shively, 2018)

In earlier exercises your POV on the other person has been simple: "My partner, who I love." This POV works for the exercise when caring is enough, but in order to progress into scene work, you need to craft a more specific and compelling POV on the *other person*. If your partner becomes a "tempting, destructive habit I just can't quit," then the relationship takes on more significance with deeper stakes. When the stakes are deep, impulses flow freely. Seeing your partner from a specific perspective makes it easier for them to pinch you. This is part of "crafting to care."

Imagine you are preparing a special picnic for a loved one. Your POV on the *other person* will change *how* you prepare that picnic. If the picnic is for your dad who is the life of the party and has always taken you on fun adventures, you might pack a frisbee and a favorite meal with a blanket that can be thrown in the back of his truck. If the picnic is for the love of your life and the person you think you're going to marry, you might pay special attention to having a beautiful blanket and a specially prepared meal so that your love will know you made it just for them. You might include a book of poetry and perhaps some flowers. What you *think* about them and how you *feel* about them affects the way you prepare the picnic for the *other person*.

This POV will also shape how you interact with them at the picnic. You might flatter both your dad and your love, but *how* you flatter them will be different because you view them differently. The POV is the meaningful lens that helps you listen specifically. The resulting pinches and tickles provoke impulses. Your impulses will then become your actions.

Bruising

Crafting the history of the relationship deepens how your *other person* pinches you. Have you ever dated someone whom you absolutely adored except for that *one thing* that is so annoying? Have you ever had a friend you loved because of that one aspect of their personality? Your sensitivity toward your shared history is what our teacher Brant would call *bruising*. When you're pinched in the same place repeatedly a bruise develops. When someone pinches that bruise it hurts even more and justifies a deeper ouch. If your dad always guilts you about how little time you spend with him, that's a bruise. If he brings up how he's glad that "you *finally* made time" for him during your special picnic, that would pinch the sensitive spot. While bruising has a negative connotation, this image of sensitivity is one we can easily relate to. If you love the way your lover looks at you when they're completely relaxed, you'll feel that pleasurable pinch on that pleasurable bruise when they look at you. It might happen while they're eating that magnificent potato salad you prepared, or while you're reading to them.

Activity #4: Independent Activity with the History of the Relationship

History of the Relationship: Going Deeper into the Imaginary World

In this section we'll focus on crafting an imaginary relationship history with your partner that culminates in you both having a clear, emotionally meaningful POV on each other. As mentioned earlier, this POV will allow your partner to pinch you more readily and cause you to ouch.

How

1. "Activity" is in their private space engaging in an Independent Activity, as you have already learned.
2. "Door" knocks and is coming for something meaningful and irreplaceable.
3. "Activity" has an expectation of who will knock on the door (not your partner), ideally one that makes "Activity" physically engage with the person at the door. Respect boundaries.
4. "Activity" opens the door while labeling the knock.
5. "Door" repeats what they hear as in previous exercises, and the exercise continues ...

Lovers or Best Friends

While a number of relationships are possible and can succeed in the exercise, we have found these two *relationship territories* to be the most dramatically useful.

A *relationship territory* is a broad starting place from which to craft a specific relationship that enlivens you. "Lovers" and "Best Friends" are emotionally meaningful, story-worthy relationships and are also within the understanding of most people.

The territory "Lovers" can mean current or ex as long as the relationship has not fully morphed into a different territory such as "friends." Similarly, "Best Friends" works even if there has been a betrayal within the friendship. It is also possible for one person to view the relationship as "Best Friends" and another person to view it as "Lover, Ex-Lover, or Would-be Lover." There are numerous possibilities.

Launching from either your "Lover" or "Best Friend" choice, craft a meaningful relationship together that culminates in the very *last moment* you saw the other person. The very last time you saw the other person needs to be crafted in detail because this final image of the person is critical for developing a clear, emotionally meaningful POV. This last moment should be one of conflict.

This relationship needs to be crafted in collaboration with your partner so that you are both living in the same imaginary reality. You don't have to share your ultimate POV on one another, but you must be in agreement on the last moment you saw one another along with other critical moments in the relationship history.

Zero Contact for 30 Days and Coming to the Door

The history you craft should also justify that it has been about a month since you've seen the other person (no talking, texting, or communicating). This fuels the POV in a way that moves the exercise forward. Thirty days is an optimal amount of time at this stage of the training.

At this point, we also deepen the stakes for "Door." "Door" will craft an irreplaceable physical object of high importance that has been left in the space where "Activity" lives and *justify* why it was left there. This item is important enough that "Door" is compelled to knock regardless of any discomfort that might be faced due to the imaginary relationship.

Some examples of an irreplaceable item can include:

1. A deceased brother's baseball card collection;
2. A beloved grandmother's engagement ring;
3. The sole copy of a very personal journal containing (use your imagination …).

Let's review and go over an example. Building on what you've already learned in Activities #1 through #3, ask yourself if your Relationship History:

1. Originates in the territory of "Lovers" or "Best Friends"?
2. Has a clear *very last moment* from each person's perspective that you've worked out together?

3. Culminates with a clear *POV* on the *other*?
4. Justifies about a month of zero contact?
5. Justifies "Door" coming over for the one-of-a-kind, emotionally meaningful, irreplaceable object?

Example: Crafting History of the Relationship

Below are examples of effective crafting for the history of the relationships that we have developed together: one for best friends and one for lovers. Note how we are selectively specific in our justifications. Note how the circumstances are both meaningful and reasonable.

Background

Here is a brief explanation of our everyday relationship so you can more easily see how we've crafted using our dramatic imaginations. We (Kevin and Kim) know each other in real life. Every few weeks we meet for coffee, a meal, or a drink. We have traveled together on business. We have a shared history in that we both attended the same graduate program at different times and we both teach acting. We enjoy a close, professional working relationship. We also both know one another's families, but 90% of the time we do anything together, our focus is on the work we share.

You may find yourself working with a partner you do not know well. That is great! There is so much that the two of you can craft together after finding some common ground. The examples we are including are heteronormative because of our respective identities, but in our acting studio we encourage our students to use their dramatic imaginations as they work with a variety of partners and relationship contexts.

Best Friends

In this example Kim will be "Activity" and Kevin will be "Door." Here's our crafting:

We met at work eight years ago. We had an instant bond over music and became best friends in our first year of working together. We traveled to the UK together to see some bands play at a festival. In the subsequent years, we have traveled the US for conferences, concerts, and friendly excursions doing the tourist thing. Throughout all of this travel, the friendship has been plutonic and resembled a healthy sibling relationship. Even when Kevin was transferred to another office across town, our friendship deepened and continued. Kevin was decidedly happy in his singleness, but Kim desperately wanted to get married and have children. Kevin respected Kim's desire and has supported her as she's dated various people over the years.

Kevin had a big birthday coming up and we decided to plan a month-long trip together to India with an excursion to Nepal that was a bucket list item for both of us. We took an entire year to plan the trip. We made several visits to the library, watched online documentaries and even hired a travel agent to work out some specific details so it would be really special and exactly everything we wanted. We purchased the tickets six months in advance and were planning the last-minute details as we counted down excitedly.

Five months before the trip, Kim met a man through her mom. He had a great job, was very stable and seemed to be crazy about Kim. Kim was excited to finally be in a relationship with someone who wanted to have children and would make a good father. He was also very kind. Kevin had met the new boyfriend, whose name was Marcus, and told Kim that he liked him. Secretly though, Kevin really thought Marcus was too committed to stereotypical gender roles. Kevin had decided to keep those opinions to himself because Kim was having such a good time with this new guy. Afterall, he thought, as long as it didn't change our special friendship, it really wasn't his business and he was glad she was happy in that part of her life.

The week before their long-awaited trip, Marcus proposes to Kim. Kim is over the moon and she and Kevin celebrate in style. The following week, Kevin is busy preparing for the trip and doesn't see Kim until the morning when he picks her up for the airport. As Kevin drives up, he sees Marcus's car in the driveway. Kim greets Kevin at the door with puffy eyes. She explains that she will not be able to go on the trip. Marcus has told her that if she loves him and values their upcoming marriage, she won't travel with Kevin alone. At that point, Marcus steps in and says, "It simply isn't appropriate for you two to keep traveling around like you're dating in college."

Kevin is furious, bites his tongue, and walks out the door. Kim follows him, apologizing and crying, trying to explain that this is her last chance to have children and a future with someone that she loves and she cannot give that up, even for a dream trip with her best friend. He walks to his car and won't talk to Kim. When he finally speaks, he tells her that Marcus is a selfish, controlling, dickhead. He tells her that marriage to this guy would kill her soul and that he won't stick around to watch her destroy her life. Kevin drives to the airport and takes the trip to India by himself.

Last Moment

The last words spoken were Kim saying "We can talk when you're ready to act like a grownup" as Kevin walks away from her. Kevin replied over his shoulder, "Then you're going to be waiting a really long time." In these *last moments*, Kim sees Kevin's back to her as he, still furious, flings his car door open. As Kevin gets behind the wheel, the last thing he sees is Kim turning her back on him and walking into the house.

Zero Contact for 30 Days

They have had zero contact with each other for 30 days because Kevin is in India vacationing and Kim dives into planning the perfect wedding with her fiancé.

POV

Kim's POV on Kevin in that last moment was: "The dream-killing, selfish Pollux to my Castor."

Kevin's POV on Kim during that last moment was: "My superficial sister chaining herself to an asshole."

These POVs were crafted in a way that is personally evocative to each of us. Kim's POV has significance because the Greek myth about the twins resonates with her sensibility of a friend she loves like a brother. There is a lot of love in this imagery and the adjective of "dream-killing" captures how devasting it would be to lose his friendship, but also how torn she feels in the imaginary circumstances of having to choose between love and family. Kevin, too, is using the sibling imagery which anchors him into love and the history of his relationship with Kim within the imagined circumstances. "Superficial" captures his perspective on the choice Kim makes to go forward with a marriage instead of being true to herself.

Kim's Activity

Kim is making a surprise gift for Marcus with the positive pregnancy test. This last month has been a full one. It has been amazing in that she finally gets to plan a wedding and she just discovered that she is pregnant, which is sooner than planned, but exciting nonetheless. She is thrilled to be pregnant and it is a dream come true. Since their engagement got off to a bumpy start because of the fight about the India trip, she needs Marcus to know how committed she is to their new family. She will prepare a box with the positive test and put it in two other boxes. The next box will be a box to keep pregnancy memorabilia in and it will be covered in pictures of her and Marcus when they were babies. She has printed baby pictures she got from both of their parents and will decoupage them on the box with thin craft paper. The outer box will be a wedding planning box, which will feature pictures of them since they met. They have a picture from their first date, which he took to send to her mom to thank her for introducing them. There are also pictures from their first baseball game, their engagement, a weekend getaway he planned for her (when she is pretty sure she got pregnant) and other pictures from the past five months. Since this pregnancy will speed up the wedding date, the boxes need to be perfect and she has written a script for how she will tell him about the pregnancy. If it goes perfectly, he will think of moving up the wedding date without her having to insist and he will be inspired by all of the wonderful things they have to look forward to. He will also know beyond a shadow of a doubt that she loves him and he will relax about her friendships and allow them to enrich their life together and not be threatened.

Marcus will be coming over for dinner at 5:30 and he is always on time. She got the photos printed after she got the files from her mom and future in-laws. She had to put dinner in the oven and get dressed in her dress from their first date. It is 4:30 pm and she has 30 minutes to complete the boxes and let them dry enough that she can assemble them without them sticking together. This should take about 20 minutes as long as the decoupage is thinly applied, according to the Internet. She can set the table in those 20 minutes which will leave her 10 minutes to assemble the boxes and wrap them before he arrives. She has new materials, the photos and a picture from the Internet that will serve as a template. Marcus is a stickler for excellence, and she wants it to be perfect!

Kim is using her dramatic imagination to craft this activity. Kim is a mother and can remember the feeling of finding out she was pregnant. She can also identify strongly with the excitement of a dream coming true. This activity is particularly compelling for her because setting the stage to create a perfect memory really enlivens her and she loves to surprise people. Kim enjoys celebrating significant life events.

Will this activity work? Let's review the Independent Activity checklist.

1. Something you can complete alone and in privacy? Yes.
2. Something that takes at least 10 minutes to complete? Yes.
3. Something you have or can easily get the necessary props for? I will need to print off the pictures and

purchase the decoupage and boxes. I have the paint brushes and will purchase a pregnancy test from the store.

4. Within your general understanding? Yes. I did decoupage at camp a few times as a middle schooler.

5. Genuinely difficult to accomplish so that it requires 100% of your attention? Yes. I have a template from the Internet that I want to follow and I have written a script. The pictures must tell that story perfectly, so as he opens it, I can prepare for the big reveal. It has to look beautiful so he will know how serious I am about our relationship and future. I have some experience with decoupage but the thin layer of glue is always a challenge.

6. Something that has a clear cap that you are working toward? Yes. Once they are finished, I can allow them to dry while I get dinner ready.

7. Something that has a reasonable pressure of time? Decoupage takes time in order for it to look good. This will take every minute I have, but I should be able to complete it.

8. Justified? Yes.

Kevin's Door

Kevin is coming over for a jade statue of Ganesha that he's sure he left at Kim's house during their last planning meeting. His Grandfather brought it back from his military service in India during World War II and gave it to Kevin when he graduated from college.

Prior to traveling to India, Kevin had helped his father downsize his house and move into a smaller, furnished apartment in an assisted living complex. When he returned from his vacation to India he spoke with his father over the phone. His dad expressed that everything was "fine" at the new place, but Kevin could tell by the sound of his voice that he wasn't yet comfortable in his new surroundings. He thought of his Grandfather's statue of Ganesha. He's sure his father would remember seeing it in his boyhood home, and that having it in his new place would be comforting for him. Kevin decided to surprise his dad with the statue over dinner at the facility. Kevin keeps the heirloom in a carved wooden box in his apartment. That afternoon Kevin is running a little late but wants to get to the facility before his dad leaves the dining room and starts his nighttime routine. Kevin grabs the wooden box, gets in the car, and starts driving. At a red light on the way he looks into the box and discovers that the statue is missing. He then remembers that he had taken the statue to Kim's to show her as they planned their trip. Luckily Kim's house is on the way to his dad's new place. The light turns green and Kevin decides that he'll call Kim from her driveway because it will save time. He figures he can let himself in because he knows where Kim keeps the outside key. When he parks, he notices Kim's car alone in the driveway. He parks his car, walks up to Kim's door, and knocks.

Let's review. Building on what you've learned in earlier activities, ask yourself if your Relationship History:

1. Originates in the territories of "Lovers" or "Best Friends"? Best Friends
2. Has a clear very last moment from each person's perspective? Yes.
3. Culminates with a clear POV on the other person? Yes.
4. Justifies a month of zero contact? Yes.
5. Justifies "Door" coming over for a one of kind, emotionally meaningful, irreplaceable object? Yes.

Lovers

In this example Kevin will be "Activity" and Kim will be "Door." Though this example is heterosexual, please don't feel obligated to create a heterosexual scenario.

Kim and Kevin were a couple back in graduate school. This was a "just for fun relationship" that lasted about a year-and-a-half. It was fun but never particularly serious as we were both completely focused on our training and laying the foundations for successful careers. After grad school, Kim moved to New York City and Kevin moved to Los Angeles. Our goodbye was a friendly one, and we decided to have a clean break – create really strong boundaries and to not call or write. We agreed that it would get weird if we stay in touch.

Seven years later, Kim's in a Denver rehearsal hall waiting for the first rehearsal to begin when Kevin walks into the room with his script. We discover that we've both been hired for a production at a regional theater in Denver. After the first read-through the entire cast goes out for dinner and drinks. As we catch up we discover that we are both single. Kim had taken a break from her relationship in New York before coming on the road. Kevin had recently ended an unsatisfying relationship that had been lingering for several months. We share an Uber back to actor housing and rekindle the relationship. We agree to keep it a secret from the company as we both know that just like in graduate school, this Rocky Mountain romance has an expiration date. Also, we don't want to be fuel for company gossip.

Over the nine weeks of rehearsals and the run of the show we have an idyllic, other-worldly reconnection and really fall in love with Denver and each other. We go hiking and mountain biking. We see Devo play a concert at Red Rocks. We find a rhythm in performing the show and living life together.

We also meet and reconnect with one another's families. Kim's parents always liked Kevin when we were in grad school and are thrilled that the two seem to be more serious now as full-fledged adults. Kevin's aunt comes to Denver to see the play and meet Kim. She encourages Kevin to keep the relationship going, seeing how happy the two are together. She tells him that there's nothing better than a relationship with a shared history and mutual interests.

As absurd and wonderful as it sounds, we realize that we're genuinely in love and decide that Kevin will move into Kim's place in New York after the show closes. We're both excited about being together as a couple and continuing our careers. We are adamant that our future together is not about having children or a mortgage.

Kevin moves from LA to NYC where we have an amazing three months together. Then Kim's career escalates and before we know it she is working non-stop on simultaneous projects. At the same time Kevin's career has remained steady but relatively tame, mostly jobbing out to different regional theater. When we are together Kevin makes strategic choices to put Kim and the relationship first. Despite her hectic schedule, Kim has noticed this and told Kevin how much she loves him and their relationship. One night, Kevin surprises Kim with a romantic evening and proposes. Before Kim can answer, he says that once they are married, he wants to start having children and explains how excited he is to raise them with her. Kim is shocked and sees this as the ultimate betrayal of what was agreed to so earnestly in Denver. We both get defensive and fight until 2 am when, exhausted, we decide to table the issue for later.

Last Moment

The next morning, both of us are tired. Kim leaves for work and Kevin says goodbye like any other morning. When Kim returns home, she discovers that Kevin has moved out. She calls him. Kevin answers his phone from the airport and tells her he's returning to LA and will stay with his aunt while he figures things out. He tells her: "I just can't put any more time into a relationship that doesn't have a future. Life has to be more than getting ready for the next job." Kim is shocked by his matter-of-fact tone and that he made this decision without talking to her. She says, "Well, I guess you didn't really love me after all." After a brief pause Kevin replies, "I don't think you know what love is." Kim hangs up the phone and Kevin boards the plane.

Zero Contact for 30 Days

Kevin has been in LA staying with his aunt and Kim has been working nonstop in NYC. Though Kim knows his aunt from her visit to see the show in Denver, Kim has chosen not to reach out to her or to Kevin because he should call her to apologize for his erratic and cruel behavior. Kevin is waiting for Kim to call him and apologize, which she would do if she really loves him and values their relationship. On social media we both limit our posts to professional updates. Nothing new to learn either way there.

POV

Kevin's POV on Kim in that last moment is: "The sucker punch of a lifetime."

Kim's POV on Kevin in that last moment is: "Betrayer of my soul."

We developed these POVs by crafting useful details in the history of the relationship and deepening the stakes. It's important not to hurry the crafting process. It takes time to create a history that feels reasonable and true.

Though the last moment is one of conflict, love must still be present in the relationship. The more we love someone, the more potential they have to hurt or delight us deeply. "The love of a lifetime" can quickly become the "The sucker punch of a lifetime," and "The only lover of my soul" can transform into "The destroyer of my soul" in an instant. These POVs were created by understanding the POVs before the conflict, and then experiencing the changes that took place as a result of the conflict. Keep love in your POV. It's what keeps you in the room with the *other person.*

Kevin's Activity

Kevin is about to pick his Aunt Abbie up from the hospital where she recently had her hip replaced. Kevin's activity involves getting the house ready for her arrival and recuperation.

While Kevin was in NYC, his aunt's son, Sam, has been taking care of her with daily visits before and after his work on the other side of the city. Sam would typically help his mom out with routine tasks before battling the traffic the rest of the way to work in the morning, or on the way to his house in the evening. Over time this began to take a toll on Sam's family life with his wife and children, as well as his professional life at the law firm. When Kevin moved back to LA after leaving Kim, he was happy to give Sam a break and take the lead on helping Aunt Abbie.

Kevin had stayed with Abbie periodically throughout his time in LA. They have a close relationship, and Abbie was happy to let Kevin stay in the guest room when he was in between living situations. Kevin left everything there when he moved in with Kim in NYC.

The morning Kevin left Kim he called his aunt from a terminal in LaGuardia. He asked if he could stay with her for a few months while he figured out his next steps. Since moving in with Abbie, Kevin has been depressed, moody, and in general not very good company. He's been helpful in taking his aunt to medical appointments, shopping and preparing meals for her, but he hasn't been the lively conversationalist that Aunt Abbie had known him to be. She was becoming genuinely concerned for his mental health and emotional wellbeing. She confided to Sam that she thought Kevin had made a terrible decision leaving Kim the way he did and that when the time was right, she was going to tell Kevin. When Sam and Kevin took Abbie in for her surgery, Sam shared this with Kevin. Kevin heard this with concern for his aunt. Given everything she was going through with her chronic hip pain and preparing for surgery, Kevin didn't want her worrying about him. As Kevin drove back to the house, he decided that he needed to prove to his aunt that he is fine and there is no cause for concern. She needs to focus on getting better.

His aunt will be discharged at 10 am. Kevin needs to have the car at the hospital's front entrance so she can easily get in. The hospital is a 40-minute drive from his aunt's house (LA traffic) and he is getting the house ready for his aunt's return.

Kevin and his aunt have a very playful relationship. His aunt is a fan of horror movies, especially classic ones. Kevin has pictures of some classic images that he has printed and is hanging around the house in opportune places: *Psycho* shower image, Pin Head, "Here's Johnny," from the *Shining*, Jason, and so on. He's hoping to bring a smile to his aunt's face, but more significantly he needs to show her that he is emotionally well and truly appreciates everything she has done for him. Kevin will also create a "ghoulish" menu of 13 streaming, scary movie choices for his aunt to choose from as she recovers. It needs to look like something you'd see in a haunted house. He plans to organize the list into appetizers, then first and second plates, and save the campy ones like *Evil Dead 2* for dessert.

Kevin is using his imagination. He does have three real aunts and can identify with the importance and uniqueness of those relationships, but this particular relationship and events are fiction. As he crafts the activity, he goes through the checklist:

1. Something you can complete alone and in privacy? Yes.

2. Something that takes at least 10 minutes to complete? Yes.

3. Something you have or can easily get the necessary props for? I will need to print off the pictures and purchase the parchment. But I own the kid scissors and can borrow the calligraphy pen and ink well from a friend. I can easily figure out which 13 films to showcase ahead of time.

4. Within your general understanding? Yes. I learned calligraphy in college to write fancy notes to a girl-friend. Even though it's been a few years and I know I'll be rusty, I can do it.

5. Genuinely difficult to accomplish so that it requires 100% of your attention? The ghoulish menu will be tough, particularly the calligraphy. It needs to be perfect for the desired effect and also to show Abbie that I'm back to my normal self. My aunt is also a skilled artist and only my best work will impress her.

6. Something that has a clear cap that you are working toward? Yes. Once the 13th film is listed in perfect penmanship. The ink will have plenty of time to dry on my way to pick her up.

7. Something that has a reasonable pressure of time? To tape the pictures around the room, put some scary ambient sounds on the stereo, and to create the scary menu will take 26 minutes. (5 minutes to tape pictures, 1 minute to select and play scary sounds on

repeat, and 90 seconds per film.) I need to walk out the door by 9:20 am to get there on time. Being late to pick up my generous aunt would be terrible!

8. Justified? Yes.

Kim's Door

After Kevin left, Kim was distraught and poured herself into work even more ferociously. Her parents have a major anniversary coming up. She is excited to celebrate it and has cleared her schedule to get home. She and her siblings have planned a huge party and she has been tasked with creating a slide show and photo boards. Her mother LOVES photo collages and has created them for every family event imaginable, even weddings and funerals. Creating the collages is always a huge ordeal and everyone stays up all night looking through the photos together.

As Kim prepares for her trip at the end of the week, she realizes that her main family photo album got packed in a box along with some of Kevin's photo albums and he must have shipped it to LA on the day he abandoned her. The album is priceless and it cannot be shipped to NYC in time to make it before she flies home. Plus, she's not sure Kevin would even answer her phone calls and she cannot bear to talk to him after his behavior. She also doesn't want it mailed to her parents because she doesn't want them to know that she and Kevin broke up because her parents have been very concerned about her choice to remain unmarried and focused on work. It has been the source of many fights and she doesn't want anything to ruin this celebration because as her parents get older, she wants each moment to count.

Kim decides to fly to LA, get her photo album, take a few meetings while she is there, and fly home to her family for the celebration without anyone having to know about her life details. Kim purchases her ticket and texts Kevin's Aunt Abbie to set up a pick-up time. She has room in her backpack for the album and plans to get to Abbie's house at 8:30 am as agreed upon. She has set up two meetings, the first of which is at 9:30 am about 60 minutes away and she won't be able to stay, which is ideal. She isn't worried about seeing Kevin because he isn't a morning person and she knows his aunt will have the album ready.

Let's review. Building on what you've learned in earlier activities, ask yourself if your Relationship History:

1. Originates in the territories of "Lovers" or "Best Friends"? Lovers
2. Has a clear very last moment from each person's perspective? Yes.
3. Culminates with a clear POV on the other person? Yes.
4. Justifies a month of zero contact? Yes.
5. Justifies "Door" coming over for the one of kind, emotionally meaningful, irreplaceable object? Yes.

A Reminder of the How

1. "Activity" is in their private space engaging in an Independent Activity, as you have already learned.
2. "Door" knocks and is coming for something meaningful and irreplaceable.
3. "Activity" has an expectation of who will knock on the door (not your partner), ideally one that makes "Activity" engage with who they expect.
4. "Activity" opens the door while labeling the knock.
5. "Door" repeats what they hear as in previous exercises, and the exercise continues ...

Traps and Pitfalls

1. Getting bogged down in unnecessary detail during your preparation. Trying to embody too many details can clutter your mind and make the circumstances more difficult to accept. It's most effective to detail sections only to the point that is essential, justified, and reasonable. In the examples above, we are very detailed about information that relates to the relationship. We don't list out everything we did in Denver, though we do list the seminal experiences. We also don't get specific with things like which airline we fly on because we have frequent flier miles, or which friends help Kim pack up Kevin's belongings in NYC.
2. Forcing elements of your imaginary history into the exercise. Remember, the exercise is always about the truth of the moment—what your partner is doing

to you *right now*. If you're looking for opportunities to expound on how your best friend betrayed you, then you're not fully present—you're trying to control the moment. You have lost contact with the *other person*. Commit to listening with 100% of your attention and fully responding to the *other person* and what they make you do.

Example: from *Best Friends* Exercise

What follows is a condensed version of one of our examples. It is likely the exercise would go on much longer if we were to do this in class. Follow the link to see an example of the full History of the Relationship exercise.

Kevin knocks at the door:

Kim   *(Opening door.)*: Crazy knock.

Kevin: Crazy knock.

Kim: Crazy knock.

Kevin: You look frazzled.

Kim   *(Torn between Kevin and getting back to her activity)*: I look frazzled?

Kevin: You look frazzled.

Kim   *(Struggling to get the layer of decoupage paste onto the picture and box surface)*: Arg!

Kevin: Arg!

Kim: Arg!

Kevin: You're freaking out.

Kim: I'm freaking out.

Kevin: You're acting like a maniac.

Kim: *I'm* acting like a maniac.

Kevin: You're acting like a maniac.

Kim: Well, spank you very much.

Kevin: Spank me very much?

Kim: You're pissing me off!

Kevin: I'm pissing you off.

Kim *(Returning her attention to the activity)*. You're pissing me off.

Kevin. You make me feel like shit.

Kim *(Not looking at him)*: I make you feel like shit?

Kevin: Yes, you make me feel like shit.

Kim: Yes, I make you feel like shit?

Kevin: You make me feel like shit.

Kim: You're sensitive.

Kevin *(Laughing)*: Yeah, I'm sensitive.

Kim: You're not sensitive.

Kevin: I am sensitive. You're not listening.

Kim *(Still working)*: I'm not listening?

Kevin: You're not listening. *(Kevin picks up the pictures)*

Kim *(Looking at him)*: Do not touch my things.

Kevin: You're terrifying.

Kim: You're damn right I am.

Kevin *(Seeing the pregnancy test and picking it up)*: I'm damn right … You're pregnant.

Kim *(Seeing Kevin pick up the pregnancy test, reaching for it)*: That's – give that to me.

Kevin: You're grabby.

Kim *(Reaching for the test)*: Give me the stick!

Kevin:	You're pregnant!
Kim:	I'm pregnant.
Kevin:	I wanna hug you.
Kim:	You wanna hug me?
Kevin:	I wanna hug you.
Kim:	I need a hug.
Kevin	*(Hugging Kim)*: You need a hug.
Kim:	You're hugging me.
Kevin:	I'm hugging you.
Kevin:	You're gonna be a momma.
Kim	*(Feeling the tug of the activity)*: I need to get this done.
Kevin:	You're walking away from me.
Kim	*(Stuck in the middle)*: You're being needy.
Kevin:	I'm being *needy*?

Establishing Boundaries

Before we introduce the History of the Relationship, we lead partners through the *Boundary Practice* introduced in *Staging Sex* (Pace, 2020, 24–31). This exercise establishes each actors' physical boundaries and where they give their partners permission to touch them each day. Let's review the core principles we introduced in Chapter 3.

1. You are responsible for your own boundaries.
2. Your boundaries are perfect just the way they are (Pace, 2020).

3. There is a difference between crossing a boundary and feeling uncomfortable.

Reinforcing the culture of consent in the studio creates an environment where the work can be more impulsive and freer. From this point on in our classes, we utilize this kind of boundary exercise with each new pairing. Activity and scene partners often choose to include the *Boundary Practice* in their warm-up as well.

An example is available on our website. Please visit www.21CActor.com and click on Exercises.

Part II
Technique

Chapter 9

The Foundations Developed, Part 2: Preparing to Work with a Script

Introduction

When we think about how POV and *Need* work together, we are reminded of a common childhood science experiment involving vinegar and baking soda. When these two compounds are mixed, they create overflowing bubbles. This chemical reaction is similar to an effective POV mixing with *Need*. When the two mix, they create impulses.

The *History of the Relationship Independent Activity* taught you how relationships can deepen your listening. The Independent Activity connected you to what is at stake and expectation. These experiences created ruts in your psycho-physical self for POV and *Need* to fuel one another in an impulse-producing weather system. Script analysis places you at the center of this satisfying storm. Rehearsal is the lab where we experiment with and fine-tune this interplay of elements.

Adding the Script

Progressing from the Repetition Exercises and Independent Activities into the script is a critical step to developing a solid technique. This section will help you connect the dots.

Before we connect the dots, let's first review how our Meisner foundations progress:

- Other –> POV
- Reality of Doing –> Need
- Impulse –> Actions

A useful way to think about scene work is that you are doing the exercise using someone else's words. In addition to the dialog, the writer also gives you a framework of *imaginary circumstances*. You will flesh out this framework with well-crafted details that will enable you to more fully embody the weather system of the story. What you practiced throughout Part I will grow and deepen throughout Part II. Below are some additional skills and considerations that will help you work effectively.

Memorizing a Script

There is something deeply collaborative about the process of memorizing and speaking a writer's words, particularly words that were meant to be heard. In the tradition of theater, we call our practice time "rehearsal" because we are literally *rehearing* the play over and over again. Because we are re*hear*ing it repeatedly, there is also a danger that we can get stuck in *line readings* or saying things in the same manner each time we play the scene.

Some find this illusion of consistency appealing, but you need to know that it is a creative dead end. Consistency in acting quickly becomes a lifeless cliché.

When memorizing lines, it is critical to stay flexible, ready to listen and respond to your scene partner. Meisner instructed actors to learn the words mechanically, or by rote (Meisner and Longwell, 1987, 67). That means you learn the text without putting any inflection on it or deciding how you will say a particular speech. Memorize in a clear and open manner. This will keep you from getting stuck in a line reading. Readiness positions you for ultimate possibilities as you rehearse.

Memorizing by rote will help you respond truthfully to impulses and moment-to-moment behavior. It will help you avoid cliché and develop a fresh, personally unique interpretation of a role. This takes practice but will allow you to fully capitalize on the skills gained through the Repetition Exercises.

Using Stage Directions

Think of stage directions as artifacts. While you are not required to obey them, they can certainly shed light on how the original production was staged or how the writer imagined the action unfolding. Some actors mark through a script's stage directions, particularly those that point to a specific emotion. We view stage directions as useful insights, so we don't mark them out. Stage directions inform our choices, but we certainly do not feel obliged to replicate them in our acting.

A Brief Word About Character

When you embody POV, Need and Action, you create the character for the audience. Trying to "become" a character is not useful. Living truthfully under any number of imaginary circumstances is useful. When you try to "get into character," you are focusing on something outside of our definition of acting. Our Meisner-based technique empowers you to bring your authentic, one-of-a-kind self into the imaginary world – your whole keyboard of humanity. Time and again we see people portray less-interesting versions of themselves when trying to "be" the character. You are much better off committing to the importance of the *other*, the reality of doing, and to truthfully "ouching" on impulse when tickled or pinched. Character is a construct of the audience. In other words, characters exist in the minds of those watching the action. The audience member's brain unconsciously interprets the sights and sounds it perceives and creates a character.

Chapter 10
Point of View (POV)

While it's the audience's prerogative to interpret the characters they see on the stage or screen, it is the actor's job to have an opinion about everything within the given circumstances of the story. This carefully crafted opinion, or POV, fuels the actor in the imaginary world.

Let's review our definition of POV:

> A highly specific, emotionally evocative phrase that encapsulates the lens through which a character views their world, their situation or their other.
>
> (Pye and Haft, 2020)

Effectively using POV requires *specificity*. It is the well-crafted details that can enliven us the most. POV helps you listen specifically in a way that makes the pinches more profound. That in turn generates strong impulses that compel you to ouch in unique ways.

When memorably labeled, this *highly specific, emotionally evocative* phrase can live easily, deep within your guts. The lens is effortlessly there. Your thoughts quiet and you accept the choice, as easily as your foot accepts a well-fitted shoe. The choice is not really you, just like the shoe is not really you, but the choice functions as a part of you and like the shoe, you can enjoy the benefits while forgetting it is there.

Your relationship to the world, to the *other character*, or even to the doorbell will be charged and motivated without needless effort. When working with a script you need to craft clear, evocative POVs on the other characters as well as the world the writer has created.

World POV

Here are two examples of World POVs:

- Life is a shit sandwich and every day I have to take another bite.
- The world is my oyster and I am the master of my fate.

These two World POVs represent very different, dynamic ways of seeing the world. Is the world a safe and friendly place? Is the glass half full? Or is trouble lurking behind every corner? Is everyone out to get you? Which basic perspective best suits your character? Discovering how your character sees the world will inform every other relationship in a specific and useful way.

Develop a World Point of View (POV)

1. Read to understand the script. During your first reading, identify *what* is happening in the play. It's important to understand the *what* before you decide upon the *how*. At this point resist making choices

about *how* a scene should be played out. Think of this as reading the script at arm's length and simply seeing the piece as a whole, not just from your character's perspective.

2. Read the script and uncover the dramatic question. Upon your second reading, start looking for the major dramatic question, or rather, ask yourself, "this is the day when WHAT happens?" In your opinion, what is the writer trying to say with this script? Are there subjects within the story that require additional research? Read to understand the story's context. Continue to resist any urge to plan your performance.

3. Read the play to *define* your character. Read like an investigator and *define* your character. Sleuth out two important things: your character's function and your character's self-image. What function do they perform as part of the larger story? Are they the protagonist, antagonist, comic relief, messenger, ingénue? To uncover the character's self-image, start by noting each thing your character says about themselves, and what other characters say about them. Does the character state their World POV? Note their behavior when alone. Note their behavior with others. Try not to judge your character.

4. Read the script and *redefine* your character by crafting them a *Heroic POV*. Every character considers themselves the hero of their own story. No one sets out to play the jerk or the mean girl. *Justify* your character's

behavior in a way that makes your character the hero in the story. How can your character see their actions as right, natural, and necessary?

At this point you have an informed opinion about your character and are ready to craft your character's POV on the world.

In Practice: Uncle Vanya

This technique is best learned by working on real scripts. We'll use the play *Uncle Vanya* by Anton Chekhov. The play was first performed by the Moscow Art Theatre, which inspired the American acting techniques of the 20th century (Klurman, 1983). In order to tell the story, Chekhov's writing demands authentic, compelling behavior, which grows out of POV, Need and Action. You will discover that there are a number of valid choices an actor can make in *Uncle Vanya*. Another reason that we find *Uncle Vanya* useful is that the world of the play is outside of our contemporary experiences. Chekhov's focus on the struggle of the human condition helps us identify closely with many of his characters regardless of our own contemporary social contexts. Our students report that Chekhov is among their favorite experiences because it requires them to live within the circumstances which are so far removed from their own. This means we all have to read the script closely and use our imaginations deliberately.[1]

The play is written about a family in early 20th-century Russia. The title character, Vanya, lives on his late sister's estate with his mother and with his niece, Sonia, the daughter of his late sister. At this time, it was the Russian custom that the estate pass to Sonia. However, her father, a professor (Serebriakoff), funds his comfortable life in town off the proceeds from the estate. Along with a handful of characters and the local doctor, Astroff, Vanya and Sonia live a quiet country life managing the estate.

The action of the play begins shortly after Sonia's father, Serebriakoff, arrives with his much younger, beautiful wife, Helena. This disruption sets the play in motion as the men admire Helena and the women fawn over the professor. Vanya is faced with his own shortcomings and jealousies. He spends much of the play professing his love to Helena. When the professor announces that he plans to sell the estate, removing the purpose of Vanya's life and potentially robbing Sonia of her inheritance, Vanya tries to shoot him, but fails.

We will work on the scene between Helena and Sonia. If you're not familiar with the play, this would be a great time to read it. It isn't mandatory, but it's a great opportunity to practice along with us. Once you have read the play, consider again the four steps of reading text for analysis:

1. Read to understand the script. Read the text to understand *what* happens in the story. Resist any urge to decide on the *how*. Arm's-length reading.

2. Read the script and uncover the dramatic question. What requires research? What is the writer trying to say?

3. Read to *define* your character within the play. What is your character's function in the story? What do they say about themselves and others? What do other characters say about them?

4. Read to *redefine* your character from your character's perspective. *Justify* your character's behavior with a *Heroic POV*.

As you read, it's helpful to write down your observations. Here's the scene between Helena, the beautiful stepmother, and Sonia, the dutiful daughter of the estate. It occurs about halfway through the play. The two women, though close in age, appear to have very little in common.

UNCLE VANYA, Act 2 (Chekhov)
HELENA comes in and throws open the window.

HELENA. The storm is over. What delicious air! [A pause] Where is the doctor?

SONIA. He has gone. [A pause]

HELENA. Sonia!

SONIA. Yes?

HELENA. How much longer are you going to sulk at me? We have not hurt each other. Why not be friends? We have had enough of this.

SONIA.   I myself – [She embraces HELENA] Let us make peace.

HELENA.   With all my heart. [They are both moved]

SONIA.   Has papa gone to bed?

HELENA.   No, he is sitting up in the drawing-room. Heaven knows what reason you and I had for not speaking to each other for weeks. [Sees the open sideboard] Who left the sideboard open?

SONIA.   Dr. Astroff has just had supper.

HELENA.   There is some wine. Let us seal our friendship.

SONIA.   Yes, let us.

HELENA.   Out of one glass. [She fills a wine-glass] So, we are friends, are we?

SONIA.   Yes. [They drink and kiss each other] I have long wanted to make friends, but somehow, I was ashamed to. [She weeps]

HELENA.   Why are you crying?

SONIA.   I don't know. It is nothing.

HELENA.   There, there, don't cry. [She weeps] Silly! Now I am crying too. [A pause] You are angry with me because I seem to have married your father for his money, but don't believe the gossip you hear. I swear to you I married him for love. I was fascinated by his fame and learning.

I know now that it was not real love, but it seemed real at the time. I am innocent, and yet your clever, suspicious eyes have been punishing me for an imaginary crime ever since my marriage.

SONIA. Peace, peace! Let us forget the past.

HELENA. You must not look so at people. It is not becoming to you. You must trust people, or life becomes impossible.

SONIA. Tell me truly, as a friend, are you happy?

HELENA. Truly, no.

SONIA. I knew it. One more question: do you wish your husband were young?

HELENA. What a child you are! Of course I do. Go on, ask something else.

SONIA. Do you like the doctor?

HELENA. Yes, very much indeed.

SONIA. [Laughing.] I have a stupid face, haven't I? He has just gone out, and his voice is still in my ears; I hear his step; I see his face in the dark window. Let me say all I have in my heart! But no, I cannot speak of it so loudly. I am ashamed. Come to my room and let me tell you there. I seem foolish to you, don't I? Talk to me of him.

HELENA. What can I say?

SONIA. He is clever. He can do everything. He can cure the sick, and plant woods.

HELENA.   It is not a question of medicine and woods, my dear, he is a man of genius. Do you know what that means? It means he is brave, profound, and of clear insight. He plants a tree and his mind travels a thousand years into the future, and he sees visions of the happiness of the human race. People like him are rare and should be loved. What if he does drink and act roughly at times? A man of genius cannot be a saint in Russia. There he lives, cut off from the world by cold and storm and endless roads of bottomless mud, surrounded by a rough people who are crushed by poverty and disease, his life one continuous struggle, with never a day's respite; how can a man live like that for forty years and keep himself sober and unspotted? [Kissing SONIA] I wish you happiness with all my heart; you deserve it. [She gets up] As for me, I am a worthless, futile woman. I have always been futile; in music, in love, in my husband's house – in a word, in everything. When you come to think of it, Sonia, I am really very, very unhappy. [Walks excitedly up and down] Happiness can never exist for me in this world. Never. Why do you laugh?

SONIA.   [Laughing and covering her face with her hands] I am so happy, so happy!

HELENA.   I want to hear music. I might play a little.

SONIA.   Oh, do, do! [She embraces her] I could not possibly go to sleep now. Do play!

HELENA.   Yes, I will. Your father is still awake. Music irritates him when he is ill, but if he says I may, then I shall play a little. Go, Sonia, and ask him.

SONIA.   Very well.

End

Below are some notes from our close reading of the scene. (The lines are in parenthesis.)

- *There has been a fight. (HELENA: How much longer are you going to sulk at me? We have not hurt each other. Why not be friends? SONIA: Let us make peace.)*

- *Pauses – indicate behavior and the writer is trying to tell us that something is changing.*

- *There was a storm. (The storm is over.)*

- *Helena is coming into Sonia's space – to talk? To clear the air? To look for someone else? Opportunity to craft expectation.*

- *They haven't talked for weeks. (Heaven knows what reason you and I had for not speaking to each other for weeks.)*

- *Sonia's father is in the next room. (No, he is in the study.)*
- *The Doctor Astroff was here and had dinner, leaving wine behind.*
- *The two drink to seal their friendship – What does this mean?*
- *Sonia has wanted to say something for a long time.*
- *Sonia cries. Then Helena cries. (Why are you crying? Now I'm crying.)*
- *Helena says she thought she married for love, but now she understands that it was not real.*
- *Helena says she has felt accused by Sonia.*
- *Sonia says, "let us forget the past." Ending the conversation? Moving forward?*
- *Helena says, "You must trust people, or life becomes impossible." World POV?*
- *Sonia calls Helena a friend.*
- *Sonia asks Helena about her life.*
- *Helena says that she is not happy.*
- *Sonia asks Helena about the doctor.*
- *Both women have strong POVs on the Doctor. Sonia reveals her full admiration. Helena is more restrained in her praise – what is she holding back?*
- *Helena states her self-image. (As for me, I am a worthless, futile woman. I have always been futile; in music, in love, in my husband's house – in a word, in everything.)*
- *Why does Sonia laugh when Helena talks about how unhappy she is? How is this justified?*

- *Helena says she feels like playing piano – we learn that she can play – Helena hasn't played for a long time. Did she learn at conservatory?*
- *Sonia's father, Helena's husband, doesn't like music when he's ill.*

After gathering these observations, begin to work through the first three questions.

1. Read to understand the script. In the middle of the night, after a storm, Sonia and her stepmother Helena talk to one another. They share a drink. They discover that they both admire the doctor.

2. Read the script and uncover the dramatic questions. The beautiful trophy wife and the homely stepdaughter reconcile and become friends. They also connect over their shared admiration for Astroff, the doctor. This scene shows how much these women need each other and how judgment and shame get in the way. It also warns of the dangers of marrying someone without real love. Will these characters find happiness? Will they reconcile themselves to their destinies and find peace?

3. Read the play to *define* your character. Note what your character says about themselves, what others say about them and their actions. This is the outward story that the audience and other characters will see and use to define your character. These observations come from the text and by listing them, you safeguard

yourself against adding or subtracting from the author's intent.

Sonia

- Helena perceived her judgment.
- She doesn't want to dwell on how she treated Helena in the past. She has strong feelings for the doctor.
- She says that she feels ashamed or silly about her feelings for the doctor.
- Helena says to her, "What a child you are." She cannot sleep – restless?
- In the monologue before Helena enters, Sonya speaks about how the doctor makes her feel and then says, "Oh! How terrible it is to be plain! I am plain, I know it. As I came out of church last Sunday I overheard a woman say, 'She is a dear, noble girl, but what a pity she is so ugly!' So ugly!" (Chekhov, Uncle Vanya, n.d.).
- In Act I, Sonia breaks up an argument between her Uncle Vanya and grandmother. She doesn't like it when people fight.
- She follows her father indoors and asks if he would like to see the work she and Vanya have done on the property.
- At the end of the play, Sonia tells Uncle Vanya that they must go on living through their difficult lives and that when they die, God will grant them peace. Her language reveals that this life is full of suffering, but in the life after they die it will be filled with beauty and rest.

Helena

- She broaches the subject to ask Sonia to put an end to their conflict.

- She suggests they share wine to seal the reconciliation, perhaps to make the conversation flow more easily.

- She confesses she thought she was in love with the Professor when she married him but realizes now, she was not.

- She tells Sonia she has felt her accusing her (judging her).

- She is very honest when Sonia asks her questions; tells Sonia she is not happy and would have liked to have a younger husband.

- She cries when Sonia cries. (Empathetic? Open-hearted?)

- She tells Sonia not to judge her and that "One must believe the best in people or life is simply miserable." This seems like a World POV. Helena believes the best in people. What might she mean by that? There's something in this idea of believing the best in people that seems like a coping strategy.

- She tells Sonia that she likes the doctor. She goes into detail about what makes him admirable and worthy.

- She says that she is worthless and futile.

- In earlier scenes when Vanya confesses his love to her, she is direct in telling him that it is wrong, and she is someone else's wife. That she does not love him and cannot love him. Her words seem firm, but not harsh.

4. Read the play to *redefine* your character from a Heroic POV. After you have completed number 3, you can finally work to justify your character's actions. Remember, your character is the hero of their own story and therefore, their justification is heroic. Take your time and have fun as you craft your answer to this last question because that will lead you toward your character's World POV. Let's look through some potential answers.

Crafting the World POV

We all have a world view. Well written characters do too. World POV helps us live more fully in the imaginary circumstances. It helps us listen specifically in a meaningful way. Listening from your own perspective will elicit one response but listening from your character's perspective will evoke different responses. An effective World POV will also lead you toward a clear POV on the *other character* in the scene, and help you justify your character's actions from a heroic perspective.

Either of these two basic perspectives can be a useful place to start:

- Life is a shit sandwich and every day I have to take another bite.
- The world is my oyster and I am the master of my fate.

Consider these opposing World POVs. If the world seems like a dangerous place to one character, then they will always be on the lookout for someone to hurt or betray them. They will see everyone as a potential threat. To an audience, they might appear paranoid. If the other character believes the world is a generous place, then each person they encounter is a potential gift-giver and affirms the goodness of the world. To the audience, they might appear idealistic. Either of these choices, require heroic justification.

Other useful questions to ask yourself:

1. Is the world dangerous or generous for my character?
2. Does my character act from their head or from their heart?
3. Does my character believe in luck or do they believe that you make your own luck?
4. Is my character focused on people or things?

Your investigation should always be informed by the script, but it cannot be bound by the lines. Your character's actions are as important as their words. There may be contradictions between what the character says they believe, and what their actions prove they believe. For example, in the play *Uncle Vanya*, the character Helena states that, "You must trust people, or life becomes impossible." She holds onto to this potential World POV, that people are worthy of trust, even as she considers breaking her marriage vows and running away with the doctor.

Craft a specific and evocative phrase that engages you immediately and brings you into the imaginary world. You should begin this work before the first rehearsal but remain flexible so that you can collaborate well and take direction. There are often several viable choices that give you multiple avenues of exploration. Enjoy experimenting with them!

With this in mind, let's *redefine our character from a Heroic POV.*

Helena Possible World POV

- "You must trust people, or life becomes impossible" (from the script).
- "My time of happiness has passed and now making others happy will give my life meaning." "There is secondhand joy in making others happy."
- "Passion is an illusion, but righteousness gives life meaning."

Window into Our Crafting

Throughout the play, Helena's words and actions demonstrate her commitment to fidelity despite her loveless marriage. She also works to build a relationship with Sonia and to dismiss Vanya's advances. We see her wanting to believe that people, including herself, are ultimately good. We can understand how this perspective comforts her and leads her to have patience with those around her, especially Sonia and Vanya.

Helena also states that her beauty and her purpose in the world are fading. Astroff further complicates things because although Helena is attracted to him and could perhaps even imagine a future with him, running away with him would condemn her to a world of perpetual shame.

A compelling World POV will help you shape more specific POVs on the other characters, their circumstances, and perhaps even the samovar.

Sonia Possible World POV

- "God suffers with us and understands, and this suffering brings me closer to his divine love." "Suffering brings us closer to God."
- "Rest only comes in death for people like me and Vanya. Life is about suffering and then God will grant me peace." "Hard work is the way to peace."
- "We must be ever worthy for even the smallest moments of joy."

Window into Our Crafting

Sonia speaks of suffering a great deal. A number of times she is called a child or exposed to be naïve. She has lived in the country her entire life and worked on the estate with her uncle. Compared to Helena, Sonia has had very little life experience and her world is very small, so it is not surprising that she falls in love with the only single man she knows who is not a relative. Though her father rejects her, she continues to seek his approval. At the end of the play,

Sonia speaks to Vanya about their suffering and how God will reward them with beauty, rest, and peace when they die.

There are some inherent traps in playing a character like Sonia. An acting trap is something that draws our attention toward something that is not useful, such as playing the mood, the emotion, the problem, replicating, and so on. In this case, the trap might be to play the victim. Sonia does not see herself as the victim. She sees herself as devout and filled with faith. Whatever World POV you choose, the choice should enliven you to play actions and not the problem. Any of these POVs may work depending on what activates you.

POV on the Other

It is easier to craft the POV on *other characters* when you know your character's World POV. Just like working with the POV in the history of the relationship, your POV on the *other character* defines the relationship. It makes the pinches and ouches deeper. POV deepens the stakes because the *other person* becomes infinitely more important. Also, the World POV informs your POVs on circumstances and even objects.

Here are working notes on the scene POVs:

Helena on Sonia
- She's my naïve, judgey stepdaughter.
- She's my only chance at a significant, loving relationship.
- She's my chance to redeem my empty, self-focused life.

Sonia on Helena

- My lying thief of a stepmother.
- She's the sad, indulgent popular girl.
- My beautiful big sister who can teach me about love.

As you develop a POV on the *other character*, remember to craft one that has the element of love woven into it. Love connects you to the *other character*. If you do not include love, you will not be able to care enough to fully experience their pinches. This is especially important whenever playing characters in conflict. The greater the conflict, the more love is necessary to keep you in the room.

As you see in this initial crafting, there are some obvious loveless choices like "lying thief of a stepmother." This is an example of a negative choice which will ultimately lead to a dead end. Acknowledging the most obvious choices in the beginning of your process, even the negative ones, can help you recognize and avoid interpretive traps. These traps lead to cliché, problem playing, and endless punishing of the *other character*. Love makes your character the hero.

Note

1 Within our actor training program we work to use a variety of scripts from different voices and perspectives. We acknowledge that while Chekhov is an early 20th-century Russian author, this material is part of the Western theatre tradition and useful as a part of this particular study. We challenge ourselves and our students to work on pieces from contemporary voices that place each student at the center of their experience.

Chapter 11

The Foundations Developed: Need (The Organizing Principle)

Once you analyze the script and begin to craft a World POV for your character, it is time to identify the *Need*. There is a *Need* for every character in every scene. Similar terms include Objective, Motivation, Goal, Essential Action (Bruder, Cohn, and Olnek, 1986), Victory, the "Must Have," and likely many more. Here's our definition of *Need*:

> The character's unconscious desire, drive or appetite to get a particular thing that exists outside of themselves.

Need encompasses two basic elements: the desire and the *other person*. Two examples:

- "I need my sexy drug to love me as much as I love them." Here the thing outside of the character is the *other person's* "love." You can only win based on the behavior of the *other person*.
- "I need my tantrummy puppy to apologize and mean it." The thing outside of the character is the "sincere apology." You can only get it from the *other person's* words and behavior.

Awareness of the Subconscious

The *Need* has its roots in Freud's widely accepted concept of unconscious motivation (Atkinson, Atkinson, and Smith, 1987); that is, a person's (and a character's) desires are unconscious to them but still incite behavior. This thing the character unconsciously desires, what they "must have" is the *Need*. As Florence and the Machine sing "We all have a hunger" (Machine, 2018). It lives in our guts and drives us toward a goal that exists in the *other person*. The character plays actions in an effort to achieve that goal. We pursue these goals even if they are not fully reached.

It is important to accept that the actor understands the character's *Needs* but that the character is not fully aware of what they are seeking. Still, this *Need* drives the character's behaviors as they seek to satisfy this hunger. If we examine the character's actions, we will see the logic in how all these actions are efforts by the character to reach their *Need*. All characters *Need* all the time.

As actors, we get to know the character's future. We learn the words and movements the character will experience before the character would if they were a person living in real time. It is important to understand that you, the actor, are conscious of things that the character would not be conscious of if they were a real person. We rehearse so that we can "forget" that preparation and purely experience the character's life as if for the first time, again and again, performance after performance.

Why Need is Important for the Actor

- The *Need* is the organizing principle that helps you understand the arc of the character. The writer embeds *Need* into the character and that *Need* becomes the through line to the dramatic action. This work happens at brain level.
- *Need* helps you embody motivational cohesion. It connects you to a visceral experience of the desire. This is gut-level work.

When working with *Need*, actors should strive to understand it, pursue it, and embody it. Analyzing a scene effectively, crafting a workable *Need*, finetuning it in rehearsal, and then committing to it in performance – all of this takes practice. For 99 percent of actors this will be difficult to master. It is worth the effort. Once you master this skill it will take your acting to a new level of truth. If you are not part of the 1% that does this instinctively, your work will plateau. You must be able to do this if you want a fully realized acting career.

Crafting an Effective Need

An effective *Need* will:

- *Be other focused.* You must pay attention to them to experience how close or far you are from getting your *Need* met.
- *Be achievable.* It's something you can actually accomplish and therefore can fully commit to.

- *Have a cap.* Just like the Activity, a cap is that moment in the *Other* person's behavior that tells you the *Need* has been reached (Bruder, Cohn and Olnek, 1986).

Need in a Nutshell

What is the *other character's* problem and how are you going to fix it? Our teacher Brant would ask, "What fire are you putting out in the other person?" or "What fire are you lighting in the other person?" Regularly returning to this question will help keep your attention on two basic components of our craft: the importance of the other person (POV) and the reality of doing (Need). When both these elements are present, impulses are born and those give your acting its unique breath of life.

Okay, How Do I Find this Precious Need?

It's not precious, it's a process. Crafting and rehearsing a *Need* is important because it enlivens you and makes you want to commit to the imaginary circumstances. If it does less than that, then your crafting isn't finished. Still, beware of perfectionism and begin with what you have. It's better to pursue a vague *Need* than pursue nothing at all. Plus, your character's *Need* is likely to emerge and focus during the rehearsal process. Avoid analysis-paralysis. Discover through doing.

Identifying the Need

Rarely will a character state their *Need*. Most of the time it will be embedded in the script's action. It's useful to know that there are three levels of consciousness where human-beings and characters engage with *Need*:

1. What people *say* they want: what they tell others and the self-image they project to the world.
2. What people *think* they want: what they think about and say privately.
3. What people *really* want: how a person's behavior reveals both their subconscious and conscious desires.

Your character is probably not conscious of their *Need*. Their behavior tells you what they really *Need*.

Uncle Vanya Example
Helena:

World POV: Passion is an illusion but doing what is right gives life meaning.

POV on Sonia: She's my naïve, judgey stepdaughter.

Potential *Needs*:

- I need Sonia to forgive me so we can become friends.
- I need her to teach me her dignity – her purity and courage.
- I need her to accept me: the good, the bad and the ugly.
- I need her to wipe the slate clean so that we can become besties.

Needs + **POV:** I need my naïve, judgey stepdaughter to become my best friend.

Sonia:

World POV: We must be worthy for even the smallest moments of joy.

POV on Helena: The sad, indulgent popular girl/My experienced, beautiful big sister.

Potential *Needs*: First part of scene

- I need her to confess her sins.
- To be honest, admit it and apologize.
- To beg for my forgiveness.

Second part of scene

- I need her to teach me how to be a woman.
- I need her to show me how to get his love.
- I need her to promise that she will get Astroff to marry me.

Need + **POV:** I need the sad, indulgent popular girl to beg for my forgiveness./I need my beautiful big sister to teach me how to be a woman.

When working on this scene we decided that Sonia had two *Needs* and that Helena had one. So, in the first section we craft that Sonia's *Need* is to get her "sad, indulgent, popular girl to beg for forgiveness." Once that *Need* is satisfied Sonia's POV changes and a new *Need* takes over.

Sonia's POV on Helena changes because of her profound discovery that Helena believed she was truly in love when she married Sonia's father. Sonia starts seeing Helena not as "indulgent" but as one who understands Love in all its complexity. Sonia already knew that Helena effortlessly commanded the attention of men. Based on this and Helena's willingness to tell Sonia the candid truth about her marriage to Sonia's father, Sonia's POV on Helena changes to "my experienced, beautiful big sister." For the remainder of the scene Sonia's *Need* is to get her "experienced, beautiful big sister to teach me how to be a woman."

From Helena's perspective, throughout the scene she sees Sonia as a naïve and judgmental stepdaughter. Still Sonia is the only woman in this play that has even a remote chance of understanding Helena, and Helena desperately wants a close female friend. Throughout the entire scene Helena is trying to strengthen this bond, to make Sonia her "bestie," and forge a true friendship. In this scene Helena *Needs* her "naïve, judgey stepdaughter to become my best friend."

Remembering that there are numerous viable choices when crafting a *Need*, let's see if the *Needs* in our example satisfy the criteria we outlined earlier.

Needs for Sonia

1. "I need the sad, indulgent popular girl to beg for my forgiveness."

- This is *other focused* because the win can only be achieved based on Helena's behavior.
- This is *achievable.* "beg for my forgiveness" is (for us) a more visceral way of saying "apologize." It is something a person can do.
- The *cap* in this situation is when Helena confesses what she has done and begs Sonia to forgive her.
- "I need my experienced, beautiful big sister to teach me how to be a woman."
- This is *other focused* because the win can only be achieved based on Helena's behavior.
- This is *achievable* because sharing secrets, insights and wisdom is something a person can actually do.
- The *cap* in this situation is when Helena teaches Sonia how to make Astroff fall in love with her.

Need for Helena

1. "I Need my naïve, judgy stepdaughter to become my best friend."
   - This is *other focused* because the win can only be achieved based on Sonia's behavior.
   - This is *achievable.* People can forge bonds and become closer.
   - This has a *cap.* When Sonia asks Helena to share her deepest secrets.

The *Needs* for Sonia and Helena in this scene are justified and actable. They are something that an actor can commit to and finetune during rehearsals.

Remember, the "foundation of all acting is the reality of doing" (Meisner and Longwell, 1987, 16) When actors are not fully engaged in doing, they end up becoming self conscious and putting their attention on things outside of our definition of acting. Crafting and committing to getting your character's *Need* met will keep you *other person* focused and doing in real time rather than focusing on your feelings, the sound of your voice, or trying to replicate that rehearsal from last week. That's a huge step forward in your craft. Congratulations!

Need in Process

It is typical to begin rehearsals with a more general idea of your character's *Need* than what you will craft by the end of the process. This is normal, especially when you are learning this skill. If you find yourself becoming frustrated because a particular *Need* eludes you, don't fret. Exhale. Run the scene again pursuing a general *Need* or give yourself a different rehearsal goal such as embracing your POV or fully ouching when pinched.

When people toil about the *Need* they are no longer using their rehearsal time effectively. Toiling is the futile, possibly compulsive insistence that you find the "right" answer immediately. When you're bogged down in toiling, you are practicing something that is not acting. By putting your attention on a different rehearsal goal and relieving the pressure to find the *Need* right now, you are more likely to discover it or finetune it through the doing.

Some general *Needs* we've found useful to get the process started:

- Getting the *other* to love or accept you the way you need to be loved or accepted.
- Getting the *other* to accept you or love you for who you really are.
- Getting the *other* to embrace change.
- Convincing the *other* to preserve a way of life.

Needs Can Change

Below are some of the reasons that cause a *Need* to change:

1. A new character enters the space. The *Need* the character is unconsciously pursuing with their best friend changes when their romantic soulmate enters the space. This is because the character's *focus* has changed. The character finds their romantic soulmate more compelling than their best friend and therefore shifts their attention from one *character* to a new *character*.

2. Profound discovery. New information becomes available that changes the character's POV on the

other character. The "problem" in the *other character* is then perceived differently and their *Need* changes as well. We saw this with Sonia in our *Uncle Vanya* example.

3. The Need is fulfilled. Once a *Need* is met, a new *Need* immediately emerges. We humans are chronically seeking creatures. Well-written characters are too.

Playing the Positive vs Playing the Problem (Pope, 2000)

"Playing the Positive" is when the actor is trying to solve the character's problem so that their *Need* is met. This is necessary and useful for actors and this is something you can commit to doing. If you need to paint a wall you want to do so effectively. You will know you're finished when the wall is completely painted, the painter's tape is removed, supplies cleaned and put away, and the paint has dried. A *Need* you might pursue in a scene is to "get an apology." This *Need* is met when the other character gives you a sincere, full apology. Both of these examples seek positive things. They both effectively solve problems.

"Playing the Positive" is the opposite of a common trap appropriately called "Playing the Problem." When an actor "plays the problem" they appear untruthful because they're not trying to solve the character's problems. Problem playing is outside of our definition of acting because the actors are either trying to demonstrate emotion or they are judging their character. Demonstrating and judging are not part of acting.

When we fall into "Playing the Problem" we are flinging paint all over the furniture rather than painting a wall. When "Playing the Problem" you're showing how "upset" you are rather than trying to fix the situation by getting the *other character* to sincerely apologize. This is also referred to as playing the emotion, mood, or a state of being. "Playing the Positive" is pursuing a *Need* that fixes the problem in the other person. It is an *effective* choice (Pope, 2000, 156).

The Need Is Not the Activity

The activity is conscious for the character. They are aware of what they are doing. When the character is decorating a cake for their nephew, they are aware of what they are doing. When the *other person* enters the space, an unconscious *Need* immediately emerges within each character that can only be satisfied outside of themselves and from the other character.

Two examples of activities that can be related to *Need*:

1. Getting a surprise special evening ready for a would-be lover: the activity is part of accomplishing the *Need* of getting the person to love you back.
2. Asking your boss for a raise: wanting the raise brings you into the room but the *Need* is what the raise

represents – the respect and validation from someone in authority or being compensated for a high level of work that makes you feel more valued than your co-workers.

POV and *Need* combine like elements to produce a chemical reaction of impulses. Shaping these impulses into actions is the final step of our process.

Chapter 12
The Foundations Developed: Action (The Actor's Tools)

In the Reality of Doing chapter you learned that doings can be directed toward objects or directed toward the *other character*. In our Part 1 Activity Exercises you learned how to commit to really doing something genuinely difficult directed toward objects. When the *other person* entered the exercise the two of you engaged in repetition, listening for pinches and impulsively ouching. When you genuinely ouch during the exercise you are freely doing actions directed at the *other person*. Impulse leads to Action. Actions are pre-meditated impulse ruts. The actor chooses actions based on the impulses discovered during the script analysis process or rehearsal. In rehearsal, the actors build the impulse ruts in pursuit of their Need. In performance, the actor impulsively responds to the *other character* with these actions.

When choosing actions, remaining flexible is key so that you can respond truthfully to the other actor and take direction. When rehearsing, be ready to shift and change as you experience the other actor's behavior. No matter the situation, choose the actions ahead of time so that you are ready to play.

Action is:

- A *doing* directed toward, and in response to, the other character in an effort to get your character's *Need* met. Additional terms for Action include tactic, verb, doing, tool, and intention.

Some common actions include flatter, threaten, shame, humor, challenge, sooth. *How* you do the action depends on your POV on the *other character* and the specific behavioral change you seek to produce in them. For example, the way you might flatter a High School cheerleader is different than how you would flatter the CEO of a large corporation because you would want each of them to behave in different ways. You might want the CEO to lean back in their big office chair and smile, while you might want the cheerleader to blush as they rush into your arms. The way you shame a parent is different than how you would shame your best friend because your POV on each is different as are the behavioral changes you're seeking to create in them too. The *how* is always dictated by the *other character* in the real-time moment and that specific change you're trying to create in them.

Actions are never any version of "being" or "seeming." "Being angry" is not an action, rather it is a state of being. "Seeming interested" is, again, a state of being and will lead to cliché or, at the least, to an actor watching themselves. These examples are outside of the definition of acting and should be avoided.

Each action is an effort toward getting your character's *Need* met. In real life a person's impulses are trying to drive them toward getting their unconscious desire satisfied. Actions are more deliberate impulse ruts chosen and rehearsed by the actor that are positive efforts to get the character's *Need* met. They are "positive" in that they are trying to solve the character's problem, not make the problem worse. Brant would sometimes refer to this as "solving energy" or "effective energy" (Pope, 2000, 156).

In the repetition your actions depended on how the *other person* was pinching you. Each ouch was justified because your impulses were a direct response to your partner's pinch. As you transition to scripted work you will label these impulses as actions and craft them into the shape of your performance. This shape becomes the rutted journey that you will be able to reexperience organically. Each time you perform, your breath, blood, and muscles will resonate with the truth of the character's journey.

Below we've added *actions (IN CAPS)* in this part of a scene from *Uncle Vanya*. Again, there are a number of viable choices. Remember that *How* the action is played is always based on the *other* person, your POV on them as well as what they are *doing* to you in the real-time moment. Your words and actions are always in *response* to something outside of yourself.

- Sonia's POV/Need: "I need my sad, indulgent, popular girl to beg for my forgiveness."
- Helena's POV/Need: "I need my naïve, judgey step-daughter to become my best friend."

UNCLE VANYA, Act 2 (Chekhov)
HELENA comes in and throws open the window.

HELENA.   The storm is over. (CORRECT) What delicious air! (HUMOR) [A pause] Where is the doctor? (HINT)

SONIA.   He has gone. (TAUNT) [A pause]

HELENA.   Sonia! (WARN)

SONIA.   Yes? (DEFY)

HELENA.   How much longer are you going to sulk at me? (DARE) We have not hurt each other. (PLEAD) Why not be friends? (CHEER) We have had enough of this. (SHAKE)

SONIA.   I myself – (LURE) [She embraces HELENA] Let us make peace. (CHALLENGE)

HELENA.   With all my heart. (INVIGORATE) [They are both moved]

SONIA.   Has papa gone to bed? (HINT)

HELENA.   No, he is sitting up in the drawing-room. (WARN) Heaven knows what reason you and I had for not speaking to each other for weeks. (TEASE)

You'll note that all these actions are actively doing something to the *other character*. You'll also notice that we have a different action for almost every sentence. This is not always the case, but it is useful to begin from the premise that each sentence, or thought, is its own unique action. Finding variety in your actions produces surprising (specific) scene work. Variety prevents predictability. How many different actions can you justify in your scene? Aim for at least six different actions.

Using a thesaurus for needless complications is a common trap. Five different words don't automatically lead to five different actions. We've found that using the simplest form of the verb is most effective for fully committing to the doing. If you have a five-sentence speech in a scene and your chosen actions are "threaten, scare, intimidate, alarm and bully," you are actually only playing one action. Look for opportunities for what we call a 180-degree shift. Where "flirt" can become "terrorize," where "menace" can become "flatter," and so on. This will help you keep the justifiable hard edges in your work that are so compelling in life. It's also a lot of fun to do!

Chapter 13
Putting It All Together

Effective rehearsal independent of a teacher or coach takes practice. Connecting your scene study technique to *Meisner-based Exercises* provides helpful guidance. Think of the scene from *Uncle Vanya* as a more structured Repetition Exercise: it's the exercise with someone else's words.

Apply what you've learned in the exercises to a script using what you know:

- The Importance of the Other Person and POV: useful bruising and heightened listening.
- The Reality of Doing and Need: recognizing and really working to fulfill your character's unconscious and conscious Needs.
- Impulse and Action: spontaneously ouching when pinched and forging Action ruts.

This process is a lot like preparing the soil to plant a garden. In order to grow certain plants, the soil needs to be optimal for the seeds to take root. When starting with a script, it is helpful to begin the process of crafting your character's POV and *Need*. If your dramatic imagination is the soil, the POV and *Need* add essential nutrients.

Next, memorize your lines by rote. Speaking and listening to the words with nothing extra put on them begins the process of organically accepting the imaginary circumstances, listening to your partner, and allowing unpressured impulses to flow. Cultivation breaks up the soil and mixes in nutrients (or amendments), taking out any weeds, rocks, candy wrappers, and anything else unnecessary. Memorizing your lines by rote with your scene partner helps you both respond impulsively to the truth of the moment.

Then it's time to test it and play with it. Can the given circumstances take root in this soil you have prepared? Getting the work on its feet is the testing ground (and playground). If impulses flow freely and can be shaped into effective Actions, then your work is on the right track and needs only slight adjustments. If you encounter bigger acting problems, then return to your crafting and make necessary changes. Common acting problems at this stage can be:

- Not caring enough about the *other character*, not listening for *pinches*.
- Not really pursuing a *Need*, not committing to the Reality of Doing.
- Playing a mood, not experiencing impulses or playing *Actions*.

Apply the Lessons of the Exercise

Embrace the Reality of Doing from the start. Use the crafting skills you developed during the Independent Activity.

For Sonia

What activity am I doing? What is the difficulty of the doing? Could you be reading one of Astroff's books so you can have a deeper conversation with him? Have you found one of Helena's romance novels and are reading it to learn how to land a man? If so, does Helena know you have her book? Or did you take it without asking and hide it when she enters? Are you knitting a scarf for your father? Struggle is dramatically interesting. What is the struggle (or difficulty) in the Activity you chose? The possibilities are endless.

For Helena

What is my activity once I enter or as I enter? The script dictates that Helena opens the window. What is the struggle (or difficulty) in this? When you combine the Reality of Doing, and reasonable struggle with the importance of Sonia you're mixing the chemicals that cause impulses to spark. Expectation: Who do you expect to enter? OR, if entering, what causes you to enter and who do you expect to see?

For Sonia

Do I hear Helena's approach? In the exercise we respond to the knock on the door and craft an expectation for reasonable surprise. Can you hear someone coming and justifiably believe it is someone other than Helena? If not, what impulses do you feel knowing that Helena is approaching? How do you expect her to behave when she arrives? The other option is to craft an expectation that it is not Helena. This surprise will fuel a reaction that will provoke you both. Both are interruptions. How do they pinch you and your activity? Pinches create impulse. Ouch on those impulses.

Expectation compels behavior. If you are knitting a scarf for your father, using a pattern that matches his beloved sweater and you think you hear his footsteps, how would you respond? Is the scarf a surprise and you need to hide it? Or is the scarf another attempt to prove your worth and you prepare to show him your fine work? Crafting your character's expectation will compel your behavior. If you are reading a romance novel that you have stolen from Helena's collection, and hear footsteps approaching, how might you behave?

For Helena

What causes me to enter and who do I expect to see? Similar to the skills you developed crafting your justification for the knock, use this opportunity to make it important and necessary rather than mundane and unjustified.

Do you know that Astroff is here having dinner and you approach wanting to see him one last time? Do you know that Sonia is here, Astroff having just left, and you come in to fix the relationship? Have your husband's digestion issues driven you from the bedroom desperate for fresh air? Having a strong justification for entering the scene gives you something to do. Does your crafting make the other person important?

For Sonia and Helena

Who is the other character to me at the top of the scene? Having a strong POV on the other character from the start makes them more important than your self-conscious thoughts. Gently place your attention on other character and allow them to change you. If you do not feel connected to the importance of the other person, how can you fix them or get them to do what you need them to do? Craft to care. Where do I experience the pinches? Test the importance of the other character.

For Sonia and Helena

Where do you experience the pinches? Once you encounter the other character, when does she pinch you? Listen for her words and behaviors to confirm or deny your POV on her and the world. Listen for signs that you are closer or farther away from achieving your *Need*. Listen for those moments to pinch you. What are the Script demands? Note external requirements.

What does the script require of you, the actor? Scripts have actions embedded in the text. Does one character interrupt the other character? Does a character cry or say "Don't touch me"? What are the external demands of the story? Exploring these requirements in rehearsal using the *pinch-ouch* moment-to-moment reality is a fun way to discover the possibilities with your scene partner. Remember that there are a number of viable choices. Resist committing too soon to that first choice. Keep exploring.

For Sonia and Helena

The script requires Sonia and Helena cry. This kind of requirement can be intimidating but, both characters have to justify the dialogue. Remember that emotions are a by-product of living truthfully under imaginary circumstances. "Forcing" yourself to cry will take you out of the moment, place your attention on yourself, and damage your performance. How can you creatively and truthfully justify the dialogue? If playing Sonia, perhaps you simply wipe your eyes and turn away from Helena. Or do you hide your face behind the book? This moment can be an obstacle for both characters as they strive to get their *Needs* met. By listening to your partner and exploring during the rehearsal process, you will find that this crying requirement can develop organically as a truthful response to the situation and what the other character is doing to you. Don't worry about the tears. Focus on the importance of the other character and getting your *Need* met. It's the fearless pursuit of *Need* with an evocative POV on the other character that creates the weather system for spontaneous impulses and emotional by-products.

Getting on Your Feet

These simple questions will help you utilize your Meisner-based skills in rehearsal. With the lines learned by rote and effective POVs and *Needs* in place, you are flexible and ready for the impulses to flow when your partner pinches you. You are now positioned to work moment-to-moment through the script and make decisions about how to shape those impulses into compelling Actions.

Part III
Additional Considerations

Chapter 14
Bigger Acting Problems

Some acting problems are not directly related to learning technique but rather are part of social conditioning or human nature. This chapter contains helpful information that addresses some of these common issues.

Replicating

Replicating remains one of the biggest acting problems we see. Replication is imitation, and while imitation is a high form of flattery, it is not acting. Our teacher Brant once said that the root of most acting hang-ups comes from actors trying to "replicate what they had seen or imagined" (Pope, 2000, 157).

We spend a lot of time-consuming images we see on screens. These visual images are then stored and become part of a catalogue in our brains. It can be tempting to replicate these images that exist in our brain catalogue, but rushing to this result is an express train to cliché and not acting. Acting should be authentic and not an imitation of someone else's work.

Sometimes we see actors engage in what we call "Original Broadway Cast Recording Syndrome," which means they are imitating someone else's performance. Miles Davis is quoted as saying, "It takes a long time to sound like yourself." Letting go of what you have seen others do can take some work, but it will pay off. There is only one you and when you behave truthfully under imaginary circumstances, no one can replicate it!

Being Stuck in Your Head

Actors often complain that they are stuck in their heads. Being stuck in your head often means you haven't spent enough time in your head, that is to say that you haven't spent enough time with the words to know them at a muscular level and you haven't spent enough time crafting through the script to understand how your *Need* and POV will produce the *Actions*.

"I need to get out of my head." That can be a major challenge 'cuz it's stuck on your neck! Kidding aside, when we say this what we really mean is that "I am thinking about things that are not useful." This almost always means that we have our attention on ourselves rather than our acting partner, or that we are not fully committing to our Needs and Actions.

To get "out of your head" start by placing your attention gently on your acting partner. Allow yourself to breathe and experience the other person. Listen to each word they say. What compels you about them in this moment? This can help you quiet your mind. Then commit to really pursuing your Need.

If you are having problems committing to the POV, Need, or Actions you've crafted then your crafting is not finished. Sleuth out the places that your common sense will not allow you to accept. Adjust your crafting so that you can accept it with the same ease and good fit of a well-designed shoe.

Over-Complicating – "So Simple Even I Could Do It"

When working on crafting in our acting class we would know we were getting close to an effective choice when Jim would say, "Now, make it so simple even I could do it." It was a useful reminder to not over-complicate. We've found that simple choices are easier to commit to and to remember during rehearsal. If what you are doing onstage is trying to remember your choices, well, then your crafting is not really complete. It is the simplest choices that become the easiest for our imaginations to accept.

Rushing to Polish – Letting It Be "Unfinished"

"Polishing" is outside our definition of acting. Our task is to "live truthfully," not to give a polished performance. Nikos Psacharopoulos (Hackett, 1996, 245) would sometimes give notes telling actors to keep their work "unfinished." This simple instruction can remind us to keep our work truthful and spontaneous, allowing it to have hard edges, rather than polishing it into something predictable and tame. We rehearse to live truthfully with the writer's words and the director's blocking. When we "set" a performance we are not acting.

Holding Your Breath

Allowing yourself to breathe easy, fully and unself-consciously will help you fully inhabit the imaginary world. This takes practice for most people. Commit yourself to a regular, healthy, and sustainable routine of stretching to develop your breathing capacity and agility.

Playing It Safe – Taking Risks

Your rehearsals will be more effective and your acting more fulfilling if you get into the habit of taking risks in your work. Remember to respect boundaries and that "actors don't bleed," but challenge yourself to take risks in every rehearsal. It is critical for cultivating impulses and doing creative work.

Boring Yourself – Making It Fun

It is important to have joy in your work. Whether embracing the ridiculous in a frivolous comedy or exploring the depths of despair in the heaviest of dramas, it is critical that you make choices that are fun for you to act. By "fun" we don't necessarily mean "happy." Instead, we mean enticing choices that excite you. When your choices make you want to jump up there and inhabit the imaginary world then you're on the right track. We regularly see the benefits of this. We also regularly see the opposite, the kind of miserable weariness that comes from routinely playing choices that are not fun. We learned this the hard way playing in repertory theatre. If we made not-fun choices, we were stuck playing them for the next four to seven months. If we made fun choices though, we got to experience that kind of inspired exhilaration night after night too. Which would you rather see? Which would you rather do?

Chapter 15
A Few Final Thoughts

Process vs. Product

We live in a world that is obsessed with products. In our opinion, one of the problems with modern capitalism is that it turns everything into a product, even people. The technique and approach covered in this book is all about process. So how do you embrace process in a product-oriented world?

To embrace process in your journey as an actor, there are some helpful things to remember. Process is messy. Meryl Streep said that "Process looks like bad acting" (Walter, 2008). Process takes time, experimentation, and refinement. Release the need to be perfect or right. Embrace curiosity.

The most effective actors have mastered the ability to play. They come to the table having done their work beforehand but hold to that work loosely. They are curious and interested in other people and don't spend their energy desperately working to appear interesting. They embrace process and continue to generate and develop ideas through that curiosity.

Books like *The Artist's Way* by Julia Cameron, *Letters to a Young Artist* by Anna Deavere Smith, and *The Creative*

Habit by Twila Tharp can help you develop a creative process. Reading biographies of well-known actors can help as well. Developing a process takes time, and by studying the process of others you will gain insight into your own.

Adjustments for Camera

The Meisner technique is often lauded as one of the most effective approaches for screen acting. We have found this to be 100 percent true. Our technique's emphasis on listening with a POV, playing actions, and experiencing impulses serves the camera well. However, we need to be cautious about becoming so dependent on the other actor that we become passive in front of the camera.

Just like stage acting requires specific craft, screen acting has the same demands. The camera does not lie and is not as forgiving as the stage. Screen acting is living truthfully under imaginary circumstances even if your partner is literally or figuratively absent. This makes a well-developed dramatic imagination and a solid acting technique crucial.

If screen acting is a passion for you, get in front of the camera as often as possible so that you can identify the ways in which your technique translates for the lens. Breath and ease stay the same in all mediums, but the camera registers ease in a more subtle way and requires that you listen freely, while having an opinion about everything. Remember that thinking is an action because the camera can see your inner monologue. The character's thought process is a major part of the storytelling on screen. Just like a long run of a play can teach you how to reserve energy for the more demanding scenes, working on camera requires a similar strategy. Looking at the shot list can help you understand the camera moves and how to reserve your energy for the close up and not spend it all on the establishing shot.

Content Creation

For centuries actors have created their own content. Even though most of the 20th century was dominated by big studios and theatre producers, today there are multiple avenues and platforms where actors can once again steer their own careers through creating content. The Internet provides a broad range of opportunities for the 21st-century actor.

Actors are dynamic creatives and usually have a hyphen in their title. Perhaps you are an actor-writer, or an actor-editor, or an actor-educator. There are endless possibilities for the skills you have. Applied Meisner can help you become a dynamic Artist-Entrepreneur. POV work is a strong foundation to create dynamic characters for a screenplay. Understanding Need can help you develop conflict in your stories. Administrative gifts can be highly creative and analysis work can lend itself to directing, producing, writing, or editing. The skills gained from a solid acting technique are what the business world calls *soft skills* and understanding your strengths within the technique can make you a dynamic member of a content creation team.

Content is a powerful form of expression. By creating your own, you fuel your creativity, build important relationships, continue to learn and grow as an artist, and share your voice with the world. Your acting technique provides a useful framework to create authentic, innovative content. There are so many stories that we still need to hear. Your story is one of them!

Giving *Other* Actors Notes

"Tend your own garden" is one of our Acting Studio Values. It doesn't matter whether your would-be note is brilliant, stupid, generous, or selfish, giving other actors notes will damage the rehearsal process and the production. When you give another actor a note you begin taking responsibility for another person's performance which puts you into the position of spectator rather than active participant. Also, when you accept a note from another actor you are relinquishing some of your responsibility for your choices and performance. Both of these things damage your acting. They also undermine your director. Best to commit to your own work and allow others to do the same.

Chapter 16
The Ethical Acting Studio

We can't begin to talk about the acting studio without talking about equity, diversity and inclusion. This work is essential if we want to build a truly collaborative, brave working space for creatives. We acknowledge the roots of white supremacy, patriarchy, and Euro-centricity embedded in the Western Theatre tradition through which our technique was established. That is why we believe it is important to actively work to disrupt the power structures that marked the 20th-century American theatre.

In the forward to his biography about the group theatre, Harold Klurman states that "ours is the only modern country which is in a state of permanent revolution" (Klurman, 1983, *The Fervant Years*). We have also experienced the acting studio in a state of necessary revolution since the beginning of the 21st century. While the acting classrooms we experienced in the 20th century were mostly white and led by male-identified teachers, we have seen training institutions undergo many welcomed changes in the past 20 years.

Typical 20th-century structures have been problematic and well-intentioned teachers have too often caused unnecessary trauma by simply following in the steps of their own teachers (replicating). We acknowledge that we have caused trauma in our own classrooms, and though it was never intentional the fact is it happened. It is our responsibility to change this problematic structure. It is our responsibility to do the work necessary so that the acting studio can be a welcoming, brave and safe place for *all* people.

The authoritarian director and acting teacher of the 20th century is giving way to a collaborative theatre artist and member of an ensemble. True ensemble teaches us the value of honor and agency for each individual in a community. New ways of working can be challenging, but in our experience, the creative freedom is worth the risk.

Our hopes for the 21st-century acting studio are aspirational, and we continue to challenge one another to make our studios more equitable and braver spaces. At the time of writing, this work has included equity, diversity, and inclusion research and training for our teaching spaces and our personal lives. It has also led us to make anti-racist training and consent-based practices a priority.

We also challenged ourselves to create innovations that would allow the technique to be more accessible to a broader and more diverse population. The technique we have put on these pages is one that has been handed down to us, a part of an oral tradition. The streamlining and codifying of it is our contribution. We expect that our students will take this technique and make it a part of themselves, which will ultimately result in new innovations. It is our hope that they will carry their own innovations of this work into their own classrooms.

Because our technique values authenticity and uniqueness, it opens up the possibility that each individual will find themselves at the center of this work. The approach that we describe gives actors agency over their process and the language and skills to articulate clear boundaries. Our work is ongoing and we are not perfect in our efforts, but we work to be transparent in our desires and we are grateful for the actors who have both held us accountable and shared their experiences where systemic power dynamics have diminished them and their work. Their contributions have led to changes and shifts within the approach outlined in these pages and continue to create more productive learning spaces.

The job of the teacher is to render ourselves unnecessary. It is a delicate balance between ego and humility to empower actors to the point where they no longer need us. We have found that actors work best in a studio where they feel valued and free to play. Our job is to hand the technique down to them so that it becomes their own. This process of developing a technique for one's self is a lifetime journey. When each student can confidently step forward into their own artistic journey, then we have done our job.

Conclusion

Beginning and ending can be a challenge. Fortunately for us, this Conclusion is not an ending. Well, sure, it is the ending of this particular book, but it is not the end of your process or ours. We wrote this book to share a workable, ethical technique that you can learn and strengthen over the course of your career. This technique empowers you to take ownership of your own creativity and craft. This book is also intended to honor our teachers, our students, our classmates, and all the actors striving to create authentically and truthfully. This book could not have been written by just one of us. We're fortunate to get to capitalize on the skills, knowledge, curiosity, lived experience, trust, and respect that we each brought to this book and to that first of many coffees. We have done our best to write a book we wish had existed when we were students in training. We have done our best to write a book that empowers the 21st-century actor with an ethical, clear, Meisner-based technique.

You have taken the time to read this text, engage with the exercises, and incorporate these techniques and sensibilities into your acting. We think you'll find your time was well spent. Re-reading this book can also help you because as you continue to develop, the way you relate to this technique will also grow. It will mature and challenge you throughout your acting career and creative life.

So, this Conclusion is also an invitation … An invitation for you to continue learning as we further develop this work and share other components and exercises that we have found useful for training 21st-century actors. If you haven't already done so, follow us on Instagram. Like us on Facebook. Subscribe to our YouTube channel. Visit our website and sign up for our mailing list so you can learn about opportunities for advanced study, acting resources, and new publications. You're also welcome to contact Kevin and Kim directly though our website. Feel free to reach out, say hello, and introduce yourself.

Now get out there and act! Practice what you've learned. Twenty-first-century stories need your unique, one-of-a-kind authenticity. Be generous and gracious to those around you. Embody your authenticity in your acting and in your art.

Your truth deserves to be heard.

Bibliography

Adler, Stella. *Stella Adler: Awake and Dream*. American Masters, Season 4, Episode 5. Director, Merrill Brockway. WNET Channel 13. July 10, 1989.

Atkinson, Rita L., Atkinson, Richard C., Smith, Edward E. and Hilgard, Ernest R. *Introduction to Psychology*. 9th ed. San Diego. Harcourt Brace Jovanovich, 1987.

Bruder, Melissa, Cohn, Lee Michael, Olnek, Madeleine, Pollack, Nathaniel, Previto, Robert, Zigler, Scott and Mamet, David. *A Practical Handbook for the Actor*. New York: Vintage Books, 1986: 13, 14, 17, 48.

Chekhov, Anton. *Uncle Vanya*. Public Domain, n.d.

Florence + the Machine. "Hunger." *High as Hope*. By Florence Welch, et al. Prod. Virgin EMI. 2018.

Hackett, Jeanie. *The Actor's Chekhov: Interviews with Nikos Psacharopoulos & the Company of The Williamstown Theater Festival*. New York: Smith and Kraus, 1996: 245.

Hagen, Uta. *Respect for Acting*. Hoboken: John Wiley and Sons, 1973.

Klurman, Harold. *The Fervent Years: The Group Theatre and the Thirties*. New York: Da Capo Press, 1983.

Meisner, Sanford and Longwell, Dennis. *Sanford Meisner on Acting*. New York: A Vintage Original, 1987: 15, 16, 35, 37, 43, 87.

Pace, Chelsea. *Staging Sex: Best Practices, Tools, and Techniques for Theatrical Intimacy*. New York: Routledge, 2020: 15, 17, 24–31, 38.

Pope, Brant. "Redefining Acting: The Implications of the Meisner Method." *Method Acting Reconsidered: Theory, Practice, Future*. New York: St. Martin's Press, 2000: 150–152, 156, 157.

Pye, Valerie Clayman and Hillary Haft Bucs. "Transformational Tactics: Engaging Students in the Heroic Pursuit of Their Objective." *Objectives, Obstacles, and Tactics in Practice:*

Perspectives on Activating the Actor. New York: Routledge, 2020: 151–152.

Shawyer, Susanne and Shively, Kim. "Education in Theatrical Intimacy as Ethical Practice for University Theatre." *Journal of Dramatic Theory and Criticism* 34.1 (Fall 2019): 87–104.

Shively, Kim. "Point of View: One Meisner Teacher's Journey to Character Development." *The Player's Journal*, 2018. Available at www.theplayersjournal.org/articles/pointofview.html.

Shurtleff, Michael. *Audition.* New York: Bantam, 1979: 36.

Theatre of War. Directed by John Walter. White Buffalo Entertainment, 2008. Available at www.kanopy.com.

Index